SU

Life for Me Ain't Been

Susan Sheehan, a staff writer for *The New Yorker,* is the
author of six previous books. *A Welfare Mother* won a
Sidney Hillman Foundation Award and *Is There No Place
on Earth For Me?* won the Pulitzer Prize for Nonfiction
in 1983. She lives with her husband, the writer Neil
Sheehan, in Washington, D.C. The Sheehans have two
daughters, Maria and Catherine.

Also by SUSAN SHEEHAN

LIFE FOR ME

AIN'T BEEN

NO CRYSTAL

STAIR

LIFE FOR ME AIN'T BEEN NO CRYSTAL STAIR

Susan Sheehan

VINTAGE BOOKS

A Division of Random House, Inc.

New York

FIRST VINTAGE BOOKS EDITION, SEPTEMBER 1994

The Library of Congress has cataloged the Pantheon edition as follows:
Sheehan, Susan, 1937–
    Life for me ain't been no crystal stair / Susan Sheehan.
    p.   cm.
    ISBN 0-679-41472-X
    1. Socially handicapped teenagers — United States — Case Studies.
    2. Teenage mothers — United States — Case studies.
    I. Title.
HVL43I.S45   1993
362.7'083 — dc20   93-18746
                        CIP
Vintage ISBN: 0-679-75450-4

Book design by Laura Hough

Manufactured in the United States of America
10   9   8   7   6   5   4   3

For Judith Green

ACKNOWLEDGMENTS

I am grateful, not for the first time, to my friends Elizabeth L. Sturz and Herbert Sturz, whom I telephoned shortly after I woke up one morning in the summer of 1990 with the idea of writing about foster care. They referred me to William J. Grinker, the commissioner of New York City's Human Resources Administration from 1986 to 1989. Bill Grinker introduced me to Poul Jensen, the assistant executive director of St. Christopher-Ottilie, the largest private foster-care agency in New York State. "If you're willing to take a ten-hour van ride from Brooklyn to Pennsylvania and back tomorrow, I promise you a subject," Poul said to me on September 17, 1990. Previous searches for book subjects had taken many months. Those words sounded auspicious. Before a van filled with St. Christopher-Ottilie child-care and social workers had even passed through New Jersey, en route to a school for delinquent boys in Pennsylvania, two of my van mates, Charlotte Bowman and Ron Underwood, convinced me that Crystal Taylor would be a perfect subject. They said she was articulate, would enjoy being written about, and would stay the course: I had told them the story I proposed to write would take a year. I had dinner with Lisa Lombardi, director of group homes for St. Christopher's, Karlaye Rafindadi, Crystal's current social worker, and Crystal on October 4th. Crystal and I liked each other from the first pina coladas we ordered. She agreed to work with me—

"It'd probably kinda help me learn my roots," she said—and did indeed stay the course, a two-and-a-half-year one, with unfailing veracity and high spirits.

In addition to those mentioned above, I am thankful to Robert J. McMahon, Nora S. Schaaf, Barbara Atkinson, Jean Canale, Connie Cantatore, Lee Cappadoro, Moneick Hancock, and Cecilia Rutledge of St. Christopher's. I am indebted to Nan Dale, Yvonne Bridges, Wendy Fieldman, Sam Turnbull, Louise Weldon, and Karen Wulf of The Children's Village; to Madelon Kendricks of Bronx-Lebanon Hospital Center; to Beverly Brooks and Dr. Merrith H. Hockmeyer of The Center for Children & Families; to Joel L. Friedman of Flushing High School; to Douglas Aymong and Joe Cullen of Satellite Academy; to Henry Ackermann of Pius XII Youth & Family Services; to Detective Joseph Gallagher of the New York City Police Department; to Dick Piperno of the Queens District Attorney's office; to David Liederman of the Child Welfare League of America; to Anne Reiniger of the New York Society for the Prevention of Cruelty to Children; to Marilyn Del Vescovo and Salvatore Costagliola of Sheltering Arms Childrens Service; to Benjamin Walker, Fred Blount, and Rochelle Wyner of Odyssey House; to Alice Boles Ott, Betsy Alterman, Muriel Leconte, and Maxine Reiss of CASA (Court Appointed Special Advocates); to Jane M. Spinak of Morningside Heights Legal Services; to Emily Stutz, formerly of The Center For Family Life; and to Jamie Greenberg, Keith Kelly, and James Smith of the New York State Department of Social Services.

Because I had the consent of Crystal, her brothers, her mother, her maternal grandmother, her son's father, and her son's foster parents, I was given access to their records at St. Christopher-Ottilie, The Children's Village, CASA, Odyssey House, and Sheltering Arms.

This book began as a two-part article for *The New Yorker*. It is a joy to have a page on which to thank some of my colleagues: Bruce J. Diones, Nicholas Parker, and Owen Phillips; Alice Mulconry, Edwin Rosario, and Stanley Ledbetter; Anne Neglia Calderera, Patricia Goering, and Felix Santos; Nancy Boensch, Patrick J. Keogh, and Christopher Shay; Judy Callender, Eleanor Gould and Joy Weiner; Ann Goldstein, Daniel Hurewitz, Louisa Kamps, and Elizabeth Macklin. Robert Gottlieb was the magazine's editor when I embarked on this odyssey. Tina Brown, its editor when the articles came in, published them with enthusiasm and (to anyone who has been on the staff of *The New Yorker* for thirty years) unprecedented and welcome alacrity. It has been my good fortune to have had John Bennet as an editor since 1981. John was the first person I called at the magazine when I decided to write about foster care and the last person to whom I talked—on a starry night from a ship that was plying its way from Hong Kong to Haiphong on the South China Sea—before going to press. He gave me the benefit of his encouragement from beginning to end.

Sonny Mehta, president of the Knopf Publishing Group, gave me the gift of a new publisher and a fine editor,

Daniel Frank of Pantheon Books. I am also indebted to Alan Turkus and to Marjorie Anderson of Pantheon.

My husband, Neil Sheehan, reads and edits everything I write before anyone else does. Every writer should be lucky enough to fall in love with and marry someone who happens to be a better writer.

My chief debt is to Crystal Taylor, her family and friends, and to the foster parents I have written about. The names of all the people in this book, including Crystal Taylor, have been changed, and identifying details have been altered. They know who they are and they have my profound thanks.

MOTHER TO SON

Well, son, I'll tell you:
Life for me ain't been no crystal stair.
It's had tacks in it,
And splinters,
And boards torn up,
And places with no carpet on the floor—
Bare.
But all the time
I'se been a-climbin' on,
And reachin' landin's,
And turnin' corners,
And sometimes goin' in the dark
Where there ain't been no light.
So boy, don't you turn back.
Don't you set down on the steps
'Cause you finds it's kinder hard.
Don't you fall now—
For I'se still goin', honey,
I'se still climbin',
And life for me ain't been no crystal stair.

—LANGSTON HUGHES

I IS LOVABLE

Crystal Taylor woke up early on Sunday morning, October 7, 1984, went to the bathroom, and noticed she was bleeding lightly. She was expecting a baby, but it wasn't due until mid-December, so she lay back down on the bed she shared with her boyfriend, Daquan Jefferson, in his parents' apartment in a Bronx housing project. Daquan's mother, Dolores Jefferson, took a look at Crystal and said, "You're getting ready to have that baby." Mrs. Jefferson couldn't bear the sight of blood. She told Crystal she didn't want her to give birth "on the outside," and, as she was leaving for church, advised Crystal and Daquan to get dressed and go to the hospital. Crystal telephoned her own mother and asked her to meet them there.

Daquan and Crystal found a taxi near the Jeffersons' building. They rode for a block while Daquan negotiated the fare with the driver. "Four-fifty," the driver said. The customary fare to Bronx-Lebanon Hospital Center was two-fifty—the amount Daquan was willing to spend. Crystal figured that the driver was asking for extra money because of her condition ("They be taking a risk that the velvet-type material they got on they seats be stained," she said later), and told Daquan, "Pay the money, pay the money." But Daquan said to the driver "Why you be charging me so much?" and then, to her, "Come on,

Crystal, I ain't letting him rob me. We got to walk and catch us another cab."

No cabs were cruising on Webster Avenue, where they got out. As they walked, Crystal kept getting contractions, and thought, I could have a baby right on a corner and this nigger beefing for two dollars. "I wanted to take him by his bony neck and strangle him," she said afterward, "but I was paining too much to be fighting." They walked about two blocks. The driver of a second taxi quoted them a fare of two dollars, and they got in. Crystal recalls that the driver drove fast and ran red lights like crazy, and that Daquan didn't even give him a tip. ("That cheap miser saved hisself fifty cents.") Her mother was waiting for her at the hospital. Florence Drummond, Crystal's mother, was on welfare. Crystal was covered by Florence's Medicaid. Crystal had been to Bronx-Lebanon once or twice for prenatal care, and was admitted as Crystal Drummond, although normally she used Taylor, her father's surname.

Crystal's mother was a heroin and cocaine addict, whose helter-skelter life her daughter often held in contempt. On that Sunday, Florence Drummond looked as if she needed a fix, but Crystal was glad to see her: Crystal, fourteen, was Florence's oldest child, and the two had usually been close. She had her mother accompany her to a labor room, and told Daquan to wait outside, because he was getting on her nerves. Each time she had a contraction, Florence told her to squeeze her hand when it hurt. The medication she was given to inhibit the contractions had no effect. Crystal was wheeled into the delivery room.

Florence held her head and told her to push. The second time Crystal pushed, Florence told her to look at the mirror on the ceiling and watch her baby as it emerged. The baby—a boy—was two months premature and had a heart murmur and slight difficulty breathing. He weighed three pounds six ounces. He was put in an incubator in the neonatal-intensive-care unit. Crystal was wheeled into a room for four.

In midafternoon, Florence went to the waiting room, where Daquan was sleeping on three chairs, shook him awake, and congratulated him on the birth of his first child. After being taken to see his tiny son, Daquan, Jr., the father, a short, dark man of twenty-three, called his own mother and ran home, still wearing a yellow hospital gown.

It had never occurred to Crystal that little Daquan—let alone Crystal herself—might end up in New York City's foster-care system. She had every intention of returning to the Jeffersons' apartment after her son's birth. If little Daquan hadn't been premature, she and Daquan would already have bought a portable crib, baby clothes, and blankets—"all that nice stuff for babies." In part because of her youth (it was hospital policy to interview all mothers below the age of eighteen), and in part because of her son's condition (he was considered a high-risk baby), a hospital social worker came to her room on Monday, October 8th. She

asked Crystal if she would be returning to her mother's residence, at 1311 Findlay Avenue—the address from which
Crystal had been admitted, and the one recorded on her son's
birth certificate. When Crystal told the social worker that her
mother was a substance abuser, who didn't have an apartment
of her own, and that she had been living with her baby's
father and his family, the social worker called the Office of
Special Services for Children, a section of New York City's
Human Resources Administration. S.S.C. assigned her and
the baby a caseworker to investigate the situation.

After listening to Crystal, the caseworker ("He was a
handsome black man," Crystal recalled later) informed her that
she and her son couldn't return to the Jeffersons'. Crystal said
she had readily consented to sexual relations with Daquan and
regarded the Jeffersons as family. She called Florence "Mommy"
and Dolores Jefferson "Ma." The caseworker said that he believed her but that his beliefs weren't relevant to her predicament. He explained that legally Crystal was still a child and
therefore was too young to consent to sex. Daquan was technically guilty of statutory rape, and might be prosecuted; his much
greater age would look bad to a judge. S.S.C. was apt to take the
position that Crystal had somehow been coerced into living
with Daquan and his family and that she and the baby could not
be allowed to live with them. In the eyes of the authorities at
the time, paternal grandparents were not the equal of maternal
grandparents: the baby's father's family had no legal responsibility for Crystal or her infant. S.S.C. *would* discharge Crystal and

little Daquan to her mother if Florence proved to be a suitable woman living in a suitable place.

The hospital put in a request for a visiting nurse to evaluate the apartment at 1311 Findlay Avenue. It was a filthy, overcrowded, underheated one-bedroom apartment rented by Florence's cousin Hazel, who shared it with her daughter, her latest man, and with Florence and the four children to whom Florence had given birth after Crystal. Hazel was also a substance abuser. Small-time drug dealers were in and out of the apartment storing and rebagging dope. Florence's youngest child, a boy born in February of 1984, at Bronx-Lebanon, had been a full-term baby, and Florence was in her thirties, so the hospital hadn't looked into her living arrangements then. Under the circumstances, S.S.C. would not permit a fourteen-year-old child and that child's child to live in such conditions. Squalor hadn't appealed to Crystal, either ("so many people sleeping in one room where everyone used to come trampeding"), nor had Hazel's two-facedness ("She smiled up in Mommy's face but when she was asleep or out she talked against her and hit up on my brothers like she did on her daughter"). Crystal had therefore packed some of her clothes in a plastic bag and had moved to the Jeffersons' a year earlier. She had returned to Findlay Avenue periodically. When Crystal was five months pregnant, Florence had called her to report that Hazel's daughter and one of her friends were wearing some clothes Crystal had left behind, and that Hazel had threatened Florence about meddling. Crystal had gone back and hit Hazel over the head with a rotten two-by-four to protect her mother. ("She ain't really got in-jured," Crystal recalls.)

Little Daquan would have to remain at Bronx-Leba-non until he weighed five pounds and was in good medical condition. Crystal was resilient and felt fine. Florence visited her every day and brought her marijuana. "She was bored," Florence says. "She had nothing further to do. Smoking weed made Crystal pleasantly high." Bronx-Lebanon needed Crys-tal's bed. She was discharged from the hospital on October 11th, four days after her admission, and was taken in a cab by the S.S.C. caseworker to the Queensboro Society for the Pre-vention of Cruelty to Children, which operated a diagnostic center where children in crisis were brought for evaluation. The caseworker said he would try to help Florence find an apartment. Until then, he would have to put Crystal in tem-porary care, and Queensboro had a bed available. Crystal cried on the way there and cried herself to sleep that night. As far as she was concerned, the diagnostic center, situated in a part of the borough of Queens given over to one- and two-family houses with front and back yards, was in the country. "I wasn't used to dirt ground or little buildings and trees," she recalls. "I was used to the city—to Harlem and the South Bronx—and to concrete and projects and high rises and stores within walking distance."

Crystal had arrived at Queensboro on a Thursday and wasn't permitted to leave the premises the first weekend. For two days, she refused to eat and kept crying. "The staffs told me to make friends with the other kids, but I was homesick," she says. "I didn't want to make friends with no strangers, I didn't want to eat they food, I didn't want to do *nothing*. I told them I had always gone to bed willingly with Daquan and I would go to bed with him willingly today. I thought my life that was just started was being ended. One nice lady staff said things wasn't as bad as they seemed, that my mother would get herself to-gether and I'd go live with her, but for now I had to live there and they were just trying to help me. She knew that when you get hungry enough you eat. That's what happened. When I came to Queensboro, I was still wearing my maternity clothes. I was soon having two plates of everything. They used no seasoning when they cooked, but I put lots of salt and pepper on my food. That stuff was good. It took me a while to get rid of my stomach and fit into my jeans."

It took Crystal less time to make friends with the other girls there—girls lived on the center's second floor—and with the boys, who roomed on the third floor and, when an alarm on the fire escape in between was set, shimmied down to the second on knotted sheets to smoke reefer and touch the girls until a counsellor caught them. "After I got to know that place, I had fun," Crystal says.

On subsequent weekends, Crystal was allowed to go to the Bronx, purportedly to stay with her cousin Hazel. She stayed with the Jeffersons. She saw her mother outside on Findlay Avenue and went to visit her son at Bronx-Lebanon every weekend.

Crystal had started drinking cheap wine and using drugs before she entered her teens, when she lived on Sheridan Avenue, in a sixth-floor walkup. Her mother had often kept her out of school to babysit two of the younger children. Crystal resented being cooped up in a hot apartment while her friends were outside playing. As a child, she liked going to school ("School was the only time I had some freedom, I could run and play"). She passed every grade through sixth despite her absences and the very scant help that Florence gave her with her homework. "I could only ask Mommy once how to do the times table," Crystal says. "If I didn't get it and asked again, she'd beat me. If I said 'Mommy, I don't think it's fair,' I got hit again. I could never express my feelings without getting a beating." Sometimes Crystal was hit for what she considered just cause— her two younger brothers ate slowly, and if she was hungry she took food off their plates—but usually not.

Florence frequently left the house at 9 A.M., saying to Crystal, "I'm going to the welfare, watch the kids, I'll be right back," and returned at 11 P.M. "I had to feed and change my brothers," Crystal says. "It was as if they were my kids. Mommy cooked a big dinner on Sunday to last two days. If I hadn't watched her cook, we'd have eaten cold foods as the week went by. I seen her wash the rice and clean the chicken and if we had chicken in the refrigerator I'd fix it for me and my brothers and leave her a plateful. Or I'd make franks and frozen French fries. We got food stamps and Mommy bought groceries with them. But we had no grownups."

When Florence was out of money, she would send Crystal to borrow food from an elderly woman who lived alone next door. The neighbor would give Crystal the two pieces of bread or the eggs she asked for, in a friendly way, but when Crystal sat outside, on a fire escape the two apartments shared, she would hear the neighbor saying to herself, "God damn it, why don't they get they own bread?" Gradually, Crystal only pretended to seek food, simulating footsteps by tapping her feet in the hall, and letting time pass until she could return to report that the neighbor had no bread. Crystal escaped the troubles of her house in various ways. She jumped from the roof of her building to the roof of the building next door and went down a flight of stairs to visit friends who lived on the fifth floor. She looked out her living-room window at the George Washington Bridge, admiring the color orange as the sun went down and night fell, and fantasized about being on a tropical island. She locked herself in the bathroom and looked at herself in the mirror. She played with her "doll babies" and a doll house she and Florence had made out of a box.

Crystal's worst single memory of her childhood is of a time when her father, Wesley Taylor, overdosed on heroin and almost died. Her parents and their friends were often in the kitchen; the children were told to stay in their room when the grownups were getting high. One evening when Crystal was about ten years old, she heard her mother screaming "Wesley! Wesley! Wesley!" She came out into the hall. Wesley was foaming at the mouth, and Florence was stuffing ice down his throat and into his pants. There were needles and bloody tissues on the kitchen table. That evening, no one else was there. Florence told Crystal to go to the building next door to get a friend. Crystal obeyed, all the while crying, "I want my daddy, I want my daddy." She remembers telling the man she was sent to summon that her father was dead and to come quick. The man tried to lift Wesley and make him walk but hadn't succeeded by the time an ambulance came. "Promise me you won't do it no more," Crystal said to her father after he returned from the hospital. "Baby girl, I ain't going to do that no more. That was a close one for me," he told her. The next night, after Wesley left to visit his mother, Felicia Taylor, Florence used up the rest of the heroin.

"I started growing hatred," Crystal says. "My father almost died and here she used that stuff and was so out of it. I thought, How stupid can you be? I was scared—I didn't know what to do if she overdosed. I said 'Mommy, you O.K.?' and she said 'I'm O.K., you go to your room.' "

When Crystal was twelve, she ran away from home for the first time, and during the seventh grade she started having trouble in school.

"I had this seventh-grade teacher, Mr. Reynolds, who had a bald spot," she says. "I came in drunk one morning. He was writing on the blackboard, and everyone was copying stuff off of it. I got up. He told me to sit down. The sun was shining on the bald spot. I went to slap the shine off of his head. I tapped him teasingly on the center of his bald spot, calling out 'Fiddle-diddle, no hair in the middle!' He chased me around the room with a pointer. I hopped over the chairs and rolled over the desks. I slapped the paperwork off of his desk, while he shouted 'You come back here!' and 'You get out of my class-room!' I was rolling on the floor trying to get away from him and the pointer and toward the exit. I leaves. In the hall, I seen the principal coming and ran the other way, to the girls' bath-room. They suspended me for two days. They made me shake Mr. Reynolds' hand and promise I'd never do that again. I managed to keep a straight face." Crystal played hooky, didn't do any homework, and didn't pass a single course that year. In the spring, she took a city-wide reading test for seventh graders: she read above grade level and was promoted.

One morning before going to the eighth grade, at Com-munity Intermediate School 147, she smoked a bag of angel dust—phencyclidine, or PCP—that she had put in Hazel's freezer the previous night to keep it fresh. When she arrived at school, she attacked her eighth-grade teacher, Mrs. Sprigg, after Mrs. Sprigg asked her a question. Crystal remembers that an assistant principal and others ("ambulance people, maybe, and cops") held her down. The next thing she remembers is waking up in Lincoln Hospital, strapped to a bed. Daquan came to the hospital with one of his brothers and two cousins, bought her a container of milk ("Milk brings the dust down," Crystal says), and took her home to her mother that evening.

Crystal was still so out of it that she didn't recognize Florence. Florence, for her part, didn't believe that her daughter had been in the hospital; she thought Crystal had been with Daquan, about whom she had mixed feelings. When Crystal first met Daquan, he was a drug dealer. He gave Florence drugs, because she seemed to expect them as her due. Crystal grew weary of her mother's freeloading and told Daquan he didn't have to get Florence high in order to date her. After Daquan stopped giving Florence drugs, her attitude toward him seemed to change. Once she became pregnant, Crystal persuaded Daquan to give up dealing in drugs, by swearing that he would never see his son if he went to jail. In September of 1984, Daquan Jefferson went on welfare, and was put to work as a custodian for the New York City Board of Education. When a permanent position opened up, he got off welfare; he has held the job ever since.

After attacking Mrs. Sprigg, Crystal gave up smoking dust. She had already given up sniffing cocaine (it had caused her to black out) and dissolving "mestabs," a pill form of mescaline, on her tongue, because "I suffers from asthma and they gave me dizzy spells." She never tried heroin ("not after seeing what it did to Mommy"), did speed, or shot cocaine ("I'm scared of needles"). Until relatively recently, she sprinkled cocaine into cigarettes and enjoyed smoking "coolies." To this day, she loves smoking marijuana, particularly in the evening and on weekends. It relaxes her, gives her a good appetite, helps her go to sleep, and makes it easier for her to have sex with the men in her life with whom she doesn't enjoy having sex.

Crystal was in the first half of eighth grade when she left Hazel's apartment. Daquan encouraged her to continue attending C.I.S. 147, which was near both Findlay Avenue and the Jeffersons' apartment. She set off for school most mornings, but she usually took the money that Daquan gave her every day for food and sundries for herself and her friends, used it to buy marijuana, met her friends in a school bathroom, and left with them for a White Castle restaurant, where she treated them to burgers. She skipped school after lunch. In eighth grade, she was very often high or absent, or both, and was well known to C.I.S. 147's truant officer. She was held back at the end of eighth grade, in June, 1984; she thinks her reading level had "sunk" as a result of too much hanging out, and she doesn't recall being present for any reading tests. By then, of course, she was pregnant. That September, she began to repeat eighth grade at Bronx Regional High School, in a special program for pregnant teenagers, which she liked. ("They served nutritious juices and everybody had a big stomach.") She had been there only a few weeks when Daquan was born. After the birth, she continued her eighth-grade studies at a special program in a Brooklyn school, to which residents of Queensboro were bused.

While Crystal was at the diagnostic center, she was questioned, tested, and evaluated by a psychiatrist, a psychologist, and a social worker. The psychiatrist noted that "her attractiveness is somewhat marred by a chipped upper front tooth." An old wino had hung out on the ground floor of 1311 Findlay Avenue. People often beat up on him. One day, Crystal was running into the building to go to the bathroom in Hazel's third-floor apartment. He thought she was running toward him to hit him, and swung the bottle he had in his hands at her—a reflex action. The bottom of the bottle cracked both her upper front teeth, one of them badly. Crystal's mother did not take her to the dentist. Both her teeth were capped after she left Queensboro.

Crystal lacked enthusiasm for tests that involved shapes like triangles, circles, and squares. "You want me to put blocks in a box?" she asked. "This is for babies." Her "Performance I.Q. Score" was ninety, but there were "indications of potential for higher functioning." A "Psychosocial Report" stated the "presenting problem" succinctly: "Child has no place to go." Her interrogators found her pleasant but depressed over her situation, which did not change as October turned to November.

By December, little Daquan weighed seven pounds, required no medication, and was overdue for discharge from the hospital. Crystal engaged in some wishful thinking—that her mother would find an apartment, and that she and her siblings would be a family again. "Not that I would have been living with her, but I could then still be living with the Jeffersons and have my baby with me in his baskinet," she recalls. But Crystal had less reason than the nice lady staff member, who knew only partial truths, to think that her mother would get herself together in the near future. Florence wouldn't come out to Queens when Crystal's caseworker called her. She made two appointments but didn't show up, saying she had no carfare. "Mommy didn't even live with Hazel," Crystal says. "She spent her nights with Clarence, the father of her last baby, in a room he rented. Day in and day out, she skin-popped heroin like she been doing since I was a toddler. I had to face the reality that Mommy getting an apartment wasn't a reality."

In mid-December, Crystal agreed to place her son voluntarily in foster care. She was crying when she signed the voluntary papers, but her S.S.C. caseworker had explained that if she didn't sign and the court took little Daquan and put him in foster care, she would have a harder time getting him back when she was older. In 1984, babies about to be placed in foster care in New York City went through an Allocations Unit. About ten percent were sent to families that had been licensed by the city and were directly monitored by employees of the city's Human Resources Administration; the rest were sent to voluntary agencies that had foster-care contracts with the city. Voluntary agencies employed their own "intake" workers (who screened and accepted children), social workers, nurses, and other personnel; their paperwork was monitored by the city.

As it happened, the family that received Daquan Drummond was affiliated with St. Christopher's Home, a Catholic agency that had been founded in 1895, in Sea Cliff, on Long Island. For most of its early years, it had served as a country home for children convalescing from surgery until their parents could care for them, and had also taken care of orphans. A year after Daquan Drummond went to St. Christopher's, it merged with Ottilie Home, a Protestant agency that also dated back to the nineteenth century. Since the fall of 1985, the agency has been called St. Christopher-Ottilie by the outside world, but within the agency it is generally called St. Christopher's. The largest number of children the agency currently serves are those in its family-foster-home-care program. Twenty-three hundred children live for a few days, a few months, or a few years with eleven hundred families of various faiths in Brooklyn, Queens, and Long Island; some are adopted by their foster parents. In late December, St. Christopher's had no places available with black foster families in Brooklyn or Queens, so on December 20, 1984, Daquan Drummond went from Bronx-Lebanon to a black family on Long Island. Black children are occasionally placed with white families, and vice versa, but it is state practice and St. Christopher's to try to place children with foster parents of the same race. As for Crystal's prospects, Queensboro, where she was staying, was supposed to house youngsters for periods of up to ninety days while doing "workups" on them, and then, with the assistance of the city's Allocations Unit, to discharge them to the most appropriate setting—a parent or parents, other relatives, foster parents, or an institution of some kind.

On January 3, 1985, Crystal was one of three girls from Queensboro who went to a St. Christopher's office in Queens to be interviewed by the director of St. Christopher's city-based congregate-care facilities. In addition to its licensed foster-care families (technically known as foster boarding homes), St. Christopher's had four small "agency-operated boarding homes" (known in the vernacular as group homes) for girls and three for boys in Brooklyn and Queens, and also a number of larger facilities in Brooklyn, Queens, and Long Island, for hard-to-place and mentally troubled children. There was one opening at a St. Christopher's group home in Queens Village. By the time Crystal returned to Queensboro, she was told that the place was hers. She was considered a good candidate for a St. Christopher's group home because she was perceived to have behaved herself at Queensboro. She had attended school every day of the week, no one had questioned what she did on weekends, she had not been caught smoking marijuana in the dorm, and she had a son in a St. Christopher's foster boarding home. Then, too, as Crystal sometimes says, "I is lovable."

The 1987 Encyclopedia of Social Work defines "foster care" as "full-time substitute care of children outside their own homes." The term includes care provided in foster homes, like the one for which little Daquan was bound, and various institutional and group settings as well, like the group home to which Crystal was going.

Before 1800, the most common form of foster care practiced in the United States was indenture, which derived from the old English Poor Laws: it provided for the forced apprenticing of dependent children until they reached the age of twenty-one. In their textbook *Child Welfare Services*, Alfred Kadushin and Judith Martin argue that after the abolition of slavery, in 1865, "it was hard to justify an indenture that required the apprehension and return to a master of a runaway apprentice."

The origin of modern foster care dates back to 1853, with the founding of the New York Children's Aid Society, by Charles Loring Brace. It developed what was called a "placing-out system." In the mid-nineteenth century, the city was faced with the problem of how to deal with approximately ten thousand vagrant children—most of them the offspring of immigrants—who were roaming the streets. Brace believed that the best way to save the children was to send them to rural areas, where farm families could put them to work in an environment regarded as morally superior to the evil urban streets. Between

1854 and 1929, a hundred thousand children from New York and other Eastern cities were rounded up and dispatched by the trainload to "free foster-family homes" in the Midwest or the South. While the younger orphan-train children were often taken in for benevolent reasons, older ones were expected to earn their keep, and one critic of placing out remarked that it was "the wolf of the old indenture philosophy of child labor in the sheepskin disguise of a so-called good or Christian home." The demise of placing out resulted from protest by the Roman Catholic Church against the placing of children in Protestant homes (most city children were Catholics) and from opposition by people in Western states to the dumping of dependent children in their midst. The practice had also come under criticism from an increasing number of child-welfare professionals.

In the late nineteenth century, another alternative was devised for hapless children. Orphanages (which dated back at least to the fourth century but were revitalized in the seventeenth and eighteenth centuries) began to be perceived as temporary homes for poor children who had become wards of the state until they could be placed in foster-family homes. In the late eighteen-sixties, Massachusetts became the first state to pay foster families board money to maintain children who might otherwise have been placed in institutions. Nevertheless, according to Kadushin and Martin, controversy raged between the advocates of institutional care and the supporters of foster-family care over which type of care was the more desirable. The first White House Conference on Children, in 1909, concluded that "the carefully selected foster home is, for the normal child, the best substitute for the natural home." This clear preference for foster-family care notwithstanding, institutional care of one sort or another continued to be the more common form provided in America in the early decades of the twentieth century, accommodating fifty-three percent of the nation's foster children as of 1933. A half century later, the proportion had declined to sixteen percent. By 1990, many child-care authorities had come to perceive the two forms of care as complementary resources. The institutions, many of which originated as orphanages, now shelter children who not only cannot live with their own families but are too disturbed to live with foster families.

The number of children in foster care declined after the passage of the Social Security Act, in 1935, because its provisions allowed more children to be financially maintained at home. The numbers began to rise again in the nineteen-sixties and seventies, as families came apart, but then declined in the nineteen-eighties, as a consequence of the Adoption Assistance and Child Welfare Act of 1980 and several other laws that attempted to control the number of children in foster care, often by helping troubled families stay together or by removing in a more timely manner children who had been placed in the system. In 1984, when little Daquan was placed in foster care, New York City's figure was 16,240, and the state's was 27,187. With the advent of crack cocaine and homelessness, the number of children in foster care took flight, and the problem also became an increasingly urban phenomenon. By 1989, there were 45,931 children in foster care in New York City and 58,540 in the state. By 1991, the numbers were 50,518 and 64,584, the latter showing New York State to have the second-highest population of foster children in the nation, after California.

In 1991, there were four hundred and thirty thousand children in foster care in the United States, at a cost of some six billion dollars, and, with more children being born each year into tenuous families or into circumstances where a child lacks even a single parent, the number seems certain to grow. In the last decade of the twentieth century, black, Native American, and Hispanic children are vastly overrepresented in foster care, and their stays tend to be longer than those of white children. Approximately eighty percent of the children coming into care are estimated to have lived with a single parent, and an increasing number of babies entering care are suffering from severe physical disabilities, notably AIDS and drug addiction. An increasing number of the adolescents in care are displaying the emotional consequences of long-term placement and multiple placements—of being moved from foster family to foster family or from foster family to institution and back, without ever really having had a place to call home.

The St. Christopher's group home to which Crystal Taylor was brought by some maintenance men from Queensboro on Friday, January 4, 1985, is a modest four-bedroom, two-story frame house on 104th Avenue, a residential block in a lower-middle-class, predominantly black neighborhood. When the group home was opened, in 1981, St. Christopher's rented the house; subsequently the agency bought it. Like St. Christopher's other group homes for girls, it houses six residents at a time, who share three bedrooms. One child-care worker covers the house from Monday morning to Wednesday afternoon, a second from Wednesday afternoon to Saturday morning, a third from then until Monday morning. This arrangement, which requires two full-time workers and one part-time worker, each of them paid hourly rates during the day and evening and a flat rate for sleeping, is the least expensive way of maintaining round-the-clock coverage. The child-care worker on duty sleeps in the fourth bedroom, which doubles as an office.

The worker who welcomed Crystal to the house immediately began to explain its regulations. No men were permitted in the bedrooms, no alcohol or drugs anywhere. Each resident was responsible for keeping her half of the bedroom tidy, for doing her laundry (there was a washer and a dryer on the premises), and for doing a rotating list of chores—cleaning the living room/dining room, the bathrooms, the kitchen, and the storage-and-laundry-room area, and taking out the garbage. A resident was given carfare, an allowance, and an opportunity to earn an extra ten dollars when it came her turn to do one of the tough jobs, like defrosting the refrigerator or scouring the stove. There were curfews—9 P.M. on week nights, and midnight or 1 A.M. on weekends, depending on age and conduct. The residents were entitled to a limited number of outgoing local phone calls a day. They were required to attend an hour-long group meeting every Tuesday evening with a psychologist, and every second Tuesday each met individually with the psychologist for twenty or thirty minutes. At Queensboro, Crystal had been given a diagnosis of "Adjustment Disorder with Mixed Disturbance of Conduct and Emotions"—a catchall diagnosis given to most youngsters seen briefly in such settings. The social worker, with whom each resident had to meet twice a month, also came to the house on Tuesdays.

Crystal was introduced to her housemates—Lynn, Yolanda, Simone, Tina, and Nicole. The five, who were between sixteen and eighteen, had been told by a child-care worker that Crystal was "a goody-goody" and had been instructed, "Do not give her no reefer."

"Do you do reefer here?" Crystal asked shortly after her arrival. She soon had Yolanda and Simone high on the supply she had brought with her. On January 11th, her fifteenth birthday, a child-care worker arranged a party for her. The worker prepared a special dinner and served ice-cream cake. Lynn and Yolanda invited friends of their own, and Crystal invited Daquan and some of his male relatives. In a group home, the youngest often becomes a scapegoat, but Lynn, the group home's leader, took a liking to Crystal, and as a result no one tried to use her as a flunky.

Three of Crystal's housemates were black, one was Hispanic, and one was half black and half Chinese. Lynn had been in foster care since birth. She had never seen her mother—a drug addict, who died when she was five—and had never known her father's surname. When she was fourteen, her foster father took her virginity, and she had been sent to the Holy Cross campus of an agency called Pius XII Youth & Family Services. Holy Cross is a residential treatment facility situated in Rhinecliff, New York; it has a school on its premises. Eighteen months later, the staff of Pius XII had decided that Lynn's behavior warranted putting her in a "less restrictive setting"—one in which she would attend public school in an urban community—and had referred her to St. Christopher's. Tina had also come to the 104th Avenue group home by way of foster care and Pius XII; Simone had come directly from a foster-care family. Yolanda and Nicole had come from home. Their mothers had felt unable to control their behavior and had petitioned Family Court for assistance; the court had deemed them "persons in need of supervision" (PINS), and they had been put in care. Before Crystal could enter the foster-care system, Florence either had to be charged with neglect—neglect can include letting a child of fourteen have a baby—or had to sign her into care voluntarily. Florence chose the latter. The specific reason stated for Crystal's placement was that her mother was homeless.

The cost of keeping a resident in a St. Christopher's group home in 1985 was about seventy dollars a day, or $25,500 a year, with most of the money going for staff salaries and for either rent or mortgage payments on the house. Every effort was made to stretch the money as far as possible. Most of the child-care workers liked to cook, and prepared breakfast and dinner. (The residents qualified for free lunches at school.) Crystal, a self-described "picky eater," considered the food at 104th Avenue excellent and ample; there was always extra food in the refrigerator and on the pantry shelves.

The group home had a small activities fund: the residents were able to go to an occasional movie, roller rink, or amusement park. They also attended Mets games on tickets regularly donated to voluntary agencies. The staff lamented the low clothing allowance—twenty-five dollars a month, plus fifty dollars a year toward a winter coat—but was resourceful about making it go as far as possible and about using the petty-cash fund when a girl had a job interview and no pantyhose without runs. One woman used a connection in the Mayor's Voluntary Action Center, to which designers donated clothes, to obtain free name-brand sportswear. She also got someone to come to the group home to show the residents surplus models of the previous year's sneakers, which they could buy for twenty-five dollars a pair instead of seventy-five dollars. Birthdays and graduations were not in the budget, but St. Christopher's workers made certain they were celebrated, because they well knew that the lives of group-home kids were lacking in celebration. (The money sometimes came out of the workers' pockets.)

To remain in the group home, each resident was required to attend school and was encouraged to work part time during the school year and full time during the summer, the better to prepare her for post-group-home life. Crystal had continued in eighth grade during her stay at Queensboro. At St. Christopher's, she was enrolled in Queens Village J.H.S. 109, the nearest junior high school. She wanted to graduate in June, so she said she had completed the eighth grade, and went into the middle of the ninth grade in January. By the time her school record caught up with her, she was doing well enough so that she was not put back. She had some difficulty with history and, later, with punctuality, and often got drunk with a girl she met in the neighborhood, but she was able to graduate in June.

At her graduation, Crystal wore a blue silk dress, high heels, and a corsage provided by St. Christopher's. Her graduation was attended by Lynn and Yolanda, several members of the staff of St. Christopher's, little and big Daquan, and Margaret and David Hargrove, the couple from Long Island who had become little Daquan's foster parents, and their daughter, Alice.

It was in the fall of 1982 that the Hargroves had made up their minds to become foster parents. Mrs. Hargrove's sister was a St. Christopher's foster mother, and the Hargroves submitted themselves to the agency's screening of prospective foster parents. They filled out a self-assessment form, provided copies of their marriage license and their latest income-tax return (in 1981, they had had a combined income of $38,627), agreed to permit the agency to make contact with their employers and to interview the people they furnished as references, and let an agency "homefinder" count and measure the bedrooms in their house—a five-bedroom Dutch Colonial in Mineola, which they had bought in 1964. The homefinder described it as "neat and well maintained inside and out" and "comfortably and appropriately decorated." They were interviewed at length. Mr. Hargrove, one of eleven children, was born in St. Croix in 1937, and Mrs. Hargrove, one of eight, in Antigua in 1942. Both had moved to New York City at early ages. He had graduated from high school; she had dropped out after tenth grade to work, and didn't "regret not having completed her schooling." They met on a basketball court in Queens in 1958, married a year later, and had two children. In 1982, their son was in the Coast Guard, and their daughter was attending college. The Hargroves' "motivation to foster children" was: "We both love children and we did so well with ours we would like to help others." Both of the Hargroves were in good health; they were Protestants but understood the state requirement that "foster parents respect the child's religion, even if different from their own"; they were willing to comply with the state and agency policy prohibiting physical punishment, and were prepared to "discipline foster children by grounding or depriving them of treats or privileges, or by talking to them." They said they understood that they were "responsible for taking a foster child to visit with his/her natural parents and siblings, as needed," and that "foster care is temporary, that the agency's goal is to reunite the family whenever possible." They had requested four children between the ages of seven and twelve who didn't have too many problems. Mr. Hargrove worked as a car salesman, a job he loved, and he expressed contentment with his life: "The only thing missing is having children in the house." Mrs. Hargrove had gone back to work once her children were in their teens. In 1982, she managed a diner from 8 A.M. to 4 P.M. and "didn't mind working but felt more fulfilled as a homemaker."

The homefinder noted that neither of the Hargroves had had an easy childhood. David Hargrove and some of his younger siblings had been under the care of their older sister, and she had yelled, punished, and hit to control them. Margaret Hargrove's mother had died when Margaret was six, and she had gone to live with an aunt, who was mean and emotionally mistreated her and her brother. The homefinder's impression was that the Hargroves would do best fostering a group of up to four siblings without severe problems, either boys or girls, ranging in age from seven to sixteen—children, essentially, in the category they had requested. "Acting out youngsters should be avoided," the homefinder wrote in a report, dated March 30, 1983. On July 1, 1983, a fifteen-year-old boy named Raymond Long and his sisters Regina, fourteen, Rosa, thirteen, and Rawanda, nine, were placed in the Hargrove home. After their mother's death in a fire, they had gone to live with their grandmother, but had proved too much for her.

In October, 1984, the agency had again called the Hargroves, to offer them two-month-old twins who needed foster care. Margaret Hargrove had by then realized that the Long children were more than she felt like handling, and she was pleased at the prospect of having infants in the house. St. Christopher's had originally certified the Hargroves for four children; it now certified them for six. The twins were taken from the Hargroves on December 7, 1984, when the court awarded custody to their maternal grandmother. "I was so upset that my mind wasn't on what I was doing and I broke the VCR," Mrs. Hargrove recalls. A few days later, St. Christopher's called again, with a two-month-old boy. Alice was home from college and answered the telephone. Mrs. Hargrove wasn't quite over the hurt of losing the twins, but Alice begged her to accept the baby, and she consented. When Crystal's S.S.C. worker brought little Daquan to the Hargroves' house, Alice opened the door. He handed the baby to her. "This is Daquan Drummond," he said. "This is for you."

For two months, Crystal Taylor considered having her

son removed from the Hargroves' home. The initial visits to see her son were to take place at a St. Christopher's office on Long Island; Mrs. Hargrove cancelled the first two visits, one of them because her car would not start on a snowy day. Margaret Hargrove took a special liking to little Daquan, and was soon bringing him to the St. Christopher's office in Queens for visits with Crystal and big Daquan. They withdrew their request to move Daquan, because they felt "comfortable" with the Hargroves. Before long, Margaret Hargrove invited Crystal to spend weekends at her home. Daquan, Sr., would often come out on Saturday or Sunday, and sometimes he and Crystal went to the movies. Crystal's social worker was enthusiastic about the visits to the Hargroves. "When Crystal is with her son, she doesn't have time to get into negative things," she wrote in Crystal's record during the summer of 1985. Crystal, however, took pleasure in negative things—primarily in returning to the 104th Avenue group home "smashed." When Mrs. Hargrove said she was eager to have Crystal placed in her home, along with little Daquan, Crystal declined, telling her, "You is terrific for my son, but you is too strict for me."

Crystal started tenth grade in the fall of 1985. Because the high school closest to the group home had a poor reputation and more than its fair share of violence, St. Christopher's was able to get Crystal accepted by Flushing High School as an out-of-zone student. Flushing High was well regarded academically and had a racially and ethnically diverse student body of about five hundred per grade. When Crystal's social worker escorted her to school the first day, Crystal expressed apprehension about attending Flushing until she spotted some boys she considered good-looking standing in front of the school building. "I think you're going to like this school after all," the social worker said.

She didn't. It was a two-bus ride to the school, the courses were challenging, and her study habits were poor. On January 11, 1986, Crystal Taylor's sixteenth birthday (shortly before she was to flunk many of her first-semester courses at Flushing), Daquan Jefferson put an engagement ring on her finger. The ring had a round fraction-of-a-carat stone in the center of a yellow-gold band, and two smaller diamonds on each side. Crystal said later that she had accompanied Daquan to a pawnshop to select it, "so's it would be satisfactory and you could see it twinkle at least a little ways off without straining your eyes or needing no magnifying glass." The ring was a bargain: Daquan paid the pawnshop a hundred dollars for it.

Soon after her birthday-and-engagement, Crystal was arrested twice. The first time was for drugs. A New York State employment program for underachievers had helped Crystal obtain a part-time job as a cashier for a grocery store. There are many activities that Crystal prefers to working, but she had been frustrated in her efforts to find employment at fast-food shops when she was fifteen, and thought she should give work a try at sixteen. Crystal had a Trinidadian friend who regularly treated her to marijuana. She wanted some reefer to celebrate her new job and went to her friend's place of business, a reefer house in Jamaica, Queens. Her friend and his cousin were at the house. They gave her some weed from one of two big bags they had concealed under a kitchen floorboard, and returned it to its hiding place. She rolled a joint and took two puffs. Before she could take a third, two police officers broke in, pointing guns and shouting "Hands up on the wall!" and "Freeze!" A police-woman patted Crystal down—Crystal had already dropped the joint—while a policeman searched the two men. Nothing was found on any of them, so the police began looking under a couch, ripped up the couch, and knocked holes in the walls with their sticks. More policemen arrived and looked harder: they pulled up the kitchen floorboard, and discovered the hidden bags of marijuana. The police suspected Crystal of being the supplier; they had had the house under surveillance when she strolled in. Asked her age, Crystal said sixteen. "Well, well, well, you just made it to go through the system," the policewoman told her. (As a minor of fifteen, who had no marijuana in her possession, she would likely have been released.) She was taken to a precinct in Jamaica to be booked. She requested the one phone call to which she was legally entitled, and was told she could call after she had been photographed and fingerprinted. Once she was fingerprinted, she was told that she was supposed to have used the phone prior to the fingerprinting, and was locked up for the night. She didn't appreciate being "suckered out" of her call. The police telephoned the group home. A child-care worker who had known Crystal since her first month at 104th Avenue drove over the following morning to take her home. She shook her head, and reminded Crystal that she had told her to stop smoking reefer countless times, and to stop hanging out with the wrong people in the wrong places. She said that she was sorry Crystal refused to use better judgment, that there could have been a shoot-out, and that, luckily, this would teach her a lesson.

Crystal went to court and refused to plead guilty. "I wasn't a carrier, I was one of the innocents," she says. "I just came to visit my friend, no harm in that, and they had no proof of wrongdoing on me." While the case was being adjourned—Crystal's Legal Aid lawyer wasn't always there to represent her—she was arrested again, for a different offense.

Crystal had continued to do poorly at Flushing High. Most days, she missed her first class. Some days, instead of going to school she and two friends from the group home travelled to Manhattan by bus and subway and went to the movies on Forty-second Street; the journey was only slightly longer than the one to school (she had complained about that journey to the group-home psychologist), and from Crystal's point of view there was more to look forward to when she reached her destination. The girls were careful not to return to the group home before the end of the school day plus an hour and a half. Crystal didn't do her homework, but once, when she was assigned by an English teacher to read a play of Shakespeare's ("That language was too much of a drag, there was too many complications," she says), she went to a movie theatre to see *Macbeth* instead. "I remember witches and a witch killed a man or a man killed a witch," she says. "It was O.K., but it was corny. It was nothing like as good as *The Wizard of Oz.*" Crystal is unfamiliar with the names of most renowned poets—Keats, Emily Dickinson, and Countee Cullen, for example—but "one day at Flushing when I decided to play student out of the many days I cut" she was exposed to a Langston Hughes poem she admired and still half remembers: "Something about an old lady looking back and telling a little boy never to give up on hisself. She said something like 'Life for me ain't been no crystal stairs, it had many boards torn up.' Because her life was not laid out on a red carpet, it made her want to do more, to get more better. It was saying to the boy even if he have to live in an apartment with no electricity, only candles, don't give up, you can always find something good at the end. I understood that poem."

One day when Crystal had attended most of her tenth-grade classes, she and two friends, Tiffany and Stacey, went to Stern's, a department store near school, in the afternoon. Each teen-ager picked out several Liz Claiborne spring outfits. They had agreed to split up and meet outside the store. Stacey put her clothes in her book bag and was apprehended as she left the store. Crystal, at sixteen, was an experienced shoplifter. When she was five or six years old, Florence often took her to "fancy department stores," like Bloomingdale's, from which Florence stole clothes to sell for drugs: a child was something of a decoy to throw off security. If Crystal needed a coat, Florence would take one off a rack, pop the ticket, and put the coat on Crystal. Most of the time, Florence just concealed the clothes she selected to "boost," over a special girdle and under her coat. Crystal was frightened when Florence was caught, arrested, and taken away for shoplifting, but she was too young to understand what the arrest was about. (She had also been frightened when Florence was arrested for welfare fraud and for selling drugs.) At eight or nine, Crystal and a group of her friends frequently stole Silly Putty and other toys from a discount store in their Bronx neighborhood. At the group home, she stole from department stores. It wasn't because St. Christopher's clothing allowance was low, or because she couldn't afford what she wanted, that she stole. Daquan gave her money regularly. Clarence, the father of Florence's youngest son, gave her fifty dollars here and a hundred dollars there. (A child-care worker who knew her well was convinced that she earned that money by going to bed with him.) Crystal stole because she calculated, "Why buy when I can just take? I can get me a new outfit and still have money in my pocket."

That particular afternoon at Stern's, Crystal didn't feel comfortable. Stacey, from the room where she was being detained, overheard the store's security personnel observing Tiffany putting the outfits she wanted in her schoolbag. When

Crystal hesitated, Tiffany handed her the schoolbag, took the clothes Crystal wanted, and put them in Crystal's schoolbag. As Tiffany walked out of the store, she got caught carrying Crystal's clothes. Crystal was caught carrying Tiffany's. The three girls were taken to a precinct in Flushing. After they were booked, they were released because none of them had ever been convicted of a crime. (Crystal's drug case was still pending.) Tiffany and Stacey called their parents, who drove to the station house to fetch them. Crystal took the Q-17 bus and the Q-2 bus back to the group home. The child-care worker on duty had already received a call from the police.

At the time, Crystal thought, Damn, those parents could have given me a ride, but, oh, well, anyway, life goes on. Once in a great while, she envied the few girls she had grown up with whose mothers didn't beat them; girls whose mothers gave them everything they wanted, including a steady supply of new clothes, and not just new clothes at the start of school, for Christmas, and for Easter, and hand-me-downs and stolen goods the rest of the year; girls who had never lived in an apartment lit by candles because the electricity had been turned off; girls whose mothers didn't embarrass them when they came to school, as Florence embarrassed her on the infrequent occasions when she was summoned, because her hands were puffy from skin-popping. (The other kids saw her hands and taunted Crystal, saying, "Your mother's a dope fiend.") And, as she grew older, she sometimes envied girls whose mothers were there for them—who had apartments, so that their daughters weren't put into foster care. Much of the time, Crystal simply acknowledged that her mother and her father, whom she hadn't seen in years, were drug addicts, who would never be the kind of family she hoped for, and, instead, looked on the bright side of group-home life.

Back at 104th Avenue, a child-care worker asked, in reference to her arrest, "Crystal, you doing it again?" and put her on a week's restriction—no use of the phone, no going out after school. Crystal handled the restriction in her fashion. She said she was going to school whether she did or didn't go, stayed out until 5 or 6 P.M., provided excuses for her tardiness (malfunctioning buses or subways, for instance), and made her phone calls before returning to the group home. "Stacey and Tiffany were probably getting preached at and punished," she says. "I knew the rules. No one at St. Christopher's could put a hand on me."

After the drug arrest, Crystal had been offered an opportunity to take advantage of the Queens District Attorney's Second Chance Program for selected first-time youthful offenders who had committed nonviolent crimes. She had maintained her innocence and had declined. But even Crystal, regarded as an expert at innocence and denial by the staff of St. Christopher's, could not deny her guilt on the shoplifting charge, so she now agreed to participate in Second Chance. Under the program, a guilty plea covered Crystal's two offenses; her criminal record would be wiped clean if she did a prescribed amount of community-service work and didn't get arrested while she was in the program or for six months afterward. If she did get arrested, she would have to face sentencing for both offenses.

Crystal was assigned to spend forty hours cleaning up Cunningham Park in Queens. She put in the hours in August of 1986, after flunking most of her courses at Flushing High. She was the only young person from Second Chance assigned to a Parks Department crew in Cunningham Park. The crew consisted of three husky men who were regular employees. Crystal, a petite, slender young woman, didn't tell them about the shoplifting charge—only about the marijuana bust, an offense to which she assumed they would be sympathetic. With a "paper-snatcher" she picked up papers left on the grass by picnickers, but she didn't care for emptying trash bins and putting new plastic bags in them. "The mens who drove the trucks could have made me work, but they were getting paid to do it, and they were nice and told me, 'Relax, relax, we got this. We'll meet you later at the basketball court,' so I worked an hour, then went off and slept and smoked a joint," she recalls. By then, Crystal was fed up with her job at the grocery store: the customers wanted their groceries packed a certain way; the fifteen-minute breaks were too short for consuming pizza. "That scene just wasn't me," she says.

In September of 1987, about six months after Crystal's arrest record was wiped clean and three months after she failed to complete tenth grade at Flushing High School for the second straight year, Crystal and her friend Tonia, from the group home, went shopping for school clothes at a mall on Long Island. Crystal had plenty of money, and spent over a hundred and fifty dollars at Macy's on an acid-washed blouse, acid-washed jeans, two Guess denim skirts, and a pair of suede moccasins. She and Tonia saw some Bill Blass and Perry Ellis socks that cost between ten and twenty dollars a pair. She thought the socks were cute but overpriced ("Socks can catch holes after you wear them a couple of times"), so she and Tonia selected a number of pairs in assorted colors and put them in their Macy's shopping bags. They didn't think anyone would be watching the sock racks. In fact, store detectives had been watching them for a long time and stopped them. They produced receipts for their purchases but had none for the stolen socks. The store detectives notified the manager, who expressed his displeasure with young black shoplifters and called the police. The girls were handcuffed and were taken to jail for the night.

Crystal's first night in jail, after the drug arrest ("City jails are casual," she says), had not intimidated her. Only her belt and her sneaker laces ("things they think you'll commit suicide with") had been removed. This time, her bra, socks, shoes, jacket, and barrettes were taken away; she was left with nothing on but her panties, pants, and a short-sleeved shirt. She was locked in a cell furnished with a bench (but no pillow or blanket), a sink, and a toilet (but no toilet paper). The mild September day became a chilly September night. Crystal was shivering, but the woman corrections officer insisted on leaving the cellblock window open. Crystal kept requesting tissues—she pretended to have a bladder problem—and the officer gave her a few at a time. Although the officer could see Crystal's cell on a television monitor and knew what she was up to, she doled out tissues for a couple of hours. By then, Crystal had used the paper to wrap her cold feet. The officer finally gave her the tissue box with the remaining tissues. Crystal put the box under her head for elevation, put her cold arms inside her shirt for warmth, and nodded off at 4 A.M. At the end of the night there was cold coffee, "nasty hard eggs on a hard roll," and another child-care worker from St. Christopher's to drive her home. Back at 104th Avenue, Crystal took a shower, threw out the clothes she had worn in jail, and went to bed. "I would have burned the clothes if I could have," she says. "I felt nasty and dirty. I felt like a whole lot had been taken from me—my self-respect, my pride. Macy's dropped the charges—I guess they figured they had taught us a lesson. I never shoplifted since. My worst fear is having to sleep in jail again. I won't steal even an eyeliner. Now if I don't have the money I do without, much as I hates doing without."

Crystal still tries to avoid doing without. A while ago, she passed a Woolworth that was having a going-out-of-business half-price sale. She went in and bought a package of mascara—Maybelline Great Lash—and some other odds and ends, like soap and Kotex. When she got home, she emptied out the Woolworth bag with her purchases, and for a minute she didn't see the mascara. When she found it, she decided to return to Woolworth the following day with her receipt to ask for the mascara that the clerk, according to her, had failed to put in her bag. She went back to Woolworth with a girlfriend, sought out the manager, told her story, and was given a replacement mascara. "For a minute, I really thought I had been done out of my Maybelline, and by the time I found it I already got the idea in my head to ask for it and there was no turning back," she told her friend. "It beats putting it in my pocket and having it taken away, and I likes beating the system honestly." Crystal's friend, a sheltered girl, who is perennially astonished by Crystal's adventures and misadventures, asked her how she had the nerve to ask the manager to replace the unmissing mascara. Her eyes narrowed merrily, and her lips widened into a grin. "My name is Crystal," she replied.

The longer Crystal remained at the group home, the less inclined she was to obey its regulations. Serving restriction for having shoplifted designer socks would have cost her too much face with Diamond Madison, a twenty-two-year-old drug dealer she had started dating a month earlier. Diamond Madison had plenty of money and was open-handed. "If he had found out, he would have said, 'What I'm going to steal for, I had the money in my pocket,'" Crystal reminisces. "He kept me in line a lot." Crystal is fickle, and most of her sexual relationships have been fleeting. Diamond is the man she has loved best so far.

By the time Crystal was four, she had been sodomized by one of her father's brothers. At twelve, she had been sexually abused by a Mr. Jones, the elderly superintendent of the last apartment Florence had in the Bronx before she was evicted for nonpayment of rent and moved in with her cousin Hazel. Mr. Jones knew that Crystal was confined to the house, taking care of her younger brothers, and that Florence beat up on her a lot, so Crystal would be grateful for a chance to get out. He told Florence that he had a sister in Harlem named Hattie who was in a wheelchair and that Crystal could clean her apartment on Sundays.

"When I got there, I saw his sister wasn't old and in a wheelchair—she was like any other old lady able to clean up her own house," Crystal says. "He made me drink liquor, he made me smoke reefer, then he made me get in the bed with him and rubbed against me. He warned me about telling my mother. He said she wouldn't believe me."

The second Sunday Crystal was taken to Harlem by Mr. Jones, she went to a store near Hattie's building. Two young men, Floyd and Keith, were on the street. Crystal was a new face in the neighborhood. When they asked who she was and she told them she was there with her uncle, Mr. Jones, they knew that she was the latest little girl Mr. Jones had lured to Hattie's apartment. "You got to stop sleeping in the bed with that old man," Crystal remembers their saying. "After eating the hamburger and French fries they bought me, I did more drinking and smoked reefer with them. Then they took me to an abandoned apartment in Hattie's building, only it was higher up. Floyd raped me while Keith watched. He then apologized, saying, 'You looked so good I couldn't help myself.' He didn't touch me again."

Floyd and Keith fed, housed, and clothed Crystal for almost two weeks, first at Floyd's girlfriend's house and afterward at a hotel. Crystal was content: she had no desire to return to her mother's building to see Mr. Jones, to do more babysitting, to absorb more beatings. Mr. Jones told Florence that Crystal had gone to the store and never come back. Florence thought that someone had kidnapped Crystal. She had separated from Crystal's father, Wesley Taylor, two years earlier, but he lived in the vicinity of Hattie's apartment. She got in touch with him, and he went out looking for her. Floyd and Keith, who were a pair of robbers, got wind of the search and turned Crystal over to a police precinct in Harlem. She was questioned, and was examined by a doctor. Mr. Jones was brought into the precinct. He denied her accusations. She was driven home in a police car. "When I got there, Mr. Jones was outside the building," she says. "He went downstairs to the basement apartment, where he lived with his wife. I went upstairs. My mother believed me in a way."

Crystal was thirteen when she met Daquan, on Findlay Avenue. On their first date, they went to the movies, had their pictures taken by a photographer outside the theatre, and went to a hotel elsewhere in the Bronx where Daquan paid for a so-called short-stay room, one they were entitled to occupy for three hours. They both smoked dust. Crystal told Daquan she was hungry—she wasn't eager to go to bed with him. He went out, and returned with "some nasty chicken." While Daquan was taking off his clothes, Crystal saw forty dollars on the floor and pocketed it. "After we had sex and done all of that, I asked Daquan for some money to buy jeans with," she recalls. "I really thought that money had been left in the hotel room by some previous person until Daquan asked me if I seen his money. I had the nerve to get down and pretend to help him look for it underneath the bed and the rug. When he realized he wasn't going to find it, we left. I told him afterwards, when we was living together, 'I robbed you. How do you think I got that extra pair of jeans?' He told me he had a feeling I took the money but he didn't want to accuse me so he ain't said nothing."

Crystal says, "I really loved Daquan, but while I was living with him I got away with having sex with another guy, Derrick, at Derrick's place. Then there was this Puerto Rican. I couldn't resist his soft lips. I had him call me at the Jeffersons'—I told him I was living with my grandmother and had an overprotective uncle but I'd be moving out soon. I went to the movies to see *Splash* with him. Daquan caught me when he brought me home, and hit me, so I never had sex with the Puerto Rican. I was two months pregnant by then."

When Crystal realized that she was pregnant, she made plans to go to a hospital clinic to verify her condition and quietly obtain an abortion. She set off for the clinic after telling Daquan she was meeting a friend before going to school. He followed her to the hospital and, unbeknownst to her, into the clinic. As the nurse's aide gave her the test results, Daquan cried out "Yes, yes, yes!" and hugged her. Crystal, who was thinking, No, no, no, felt frustrated. She cried. "My scheme had been blown." Mrs. Jefferson agreed with her son. "You don't be needing no abortion," she said. "Them things are dangerous."

While Crystal was living at Queensboro and was visiting her baby at Bronx-Lebanon at two o'clock one Sunday morning (the hospital permitted visits around the clock), Daquan came by and caught her talking to John, the guy she had been dating (but not sleeping with) when Daquan met her and won her away from him. Daquan wanted to fight Crystal that Sunday morning. "We did a lot of punching and grabbing over the years," she says. "When I was fifteen, I hit him over the head with a glass ashtray shaped like a gingerbread man. When I was on the phone with my male friends, he'd try to listen; I'd smash him over the head with the phone."

Around the time of little Daquan's birth, Crystal had told her mother how much she was in love with Daquan, her infidelities notwithstanding. She stretched out the monosyllable so that anyone hearing her would have written down "loooooove." "I give it a year after that baby is born," Florence had said. "Then tell me how much you looo-ooove him."

At sixteen, Crystal took care to leave her engagement ring in her pocket or in her dresser drawer except when she was with Daquan. "I realized I was making a fool of myself," she says. "Daquan's expectations were husband and wife and me to call him every time I got home from school. At that age, I was blossing and blooming. There was a lot of fun to be had going to roller rinks and discos with people I was meeting nearer my age, but Daquan was getting upset and asking all these questions. I was sixteen, he was twenty-five. I sat him down and told him he'd been where I was going. 'I never had a childhood, but I'm going to have a teen-agehood,' I said. 'Maybe we'll get back together when I'm older.' I dated younger guys. Their demands was less great. And they were better-looking. Daquan walks funny and his eyes is always bloodshot. I'm five feet and a half a inch, and he's shorter than that. For me, you got to be at least five-eight and built big, with lots and lots of muscles. I look at Daquan now and I ask myself, 'How the hell did I do it?' "

During Crystal's sixteenth summer, she met Richard, a student at Howard University who was home on vacation. He was tall and muscular, but, she says, "the sex wasn't there." Then, in August of 1987, she started seeing Diamond. He took her horseback riding on their first date. On later dates, they went to Coney Island and to the beach at Far Rockaway, and rode around on his red Suzuki motorcycle. They first made love in October, at the Capri, a hotel with short-stay rates near the group home. Diamond, a high-school graduate, lived with his mother, his grandmother, and his sister. Crystal and Diamond later made love, with his mother's tacit consent, in his room. "He was the best in bed, before or since, and for the year and a half before we split I was unfaithful to him only once, for five minutes," she says. Crystal becomes wistful and teary when she talks about Diamond. "No one never took me horseback riding before Diamond," she says. "It was the first time I was close to a horse. I had never gone to the beach with anyone, never looked at no moon. The water, the waves, and the sand—we raced from one lifeguard chair to the next. We put a blanket on the back of his bike and he kissed me—that man showed me some romantic times. People said, 'All them girls in the group home is ho's, let's get one of them girls and stick them.' Diamond never caught that attitude. I would go to the movies with my girlfriend, and Diamond would have a cab pick us up to take us there. He'd be busy selling drugs but he'd stop to call a cab to take us home from the movies. He made me feel good about myself."

The acid-washed blouse and jeans that Crystal had paid for at Macy's were part of her wardrobe for Satellite Academy, a school to which she would be transferring in the fall of 1987. Flushing High School had proved too "scholastic" for Crystal; her haphazard junior-high-school years hadn't prepared her for subjects like social studies, and she acknowledges that she had "a bad attitude." One day, she and two friends hung out in the corridor outside her Flushing High math classroom after the bell rang. She then knocked on the classroom door. "A classmate made an attempt to open the door, but the teacher said to sit back down," Crystal says. "So I banged on a glass pane in the classroom door and it broke. After that, the teacher hurried up and opened the door. I asked her why she ain't let me in, because I felt she had dissed me. She told me not to worry, she wasn't going to write me up this time, just take a seat. The bitch was scared. At the end of the class, she wrote out a memo for maintenance to sweep up the glass and replace the pane. I turned myself in to the dean after that incident, and she said 'Don't worry about it.' That was only because she couldn't put nothing in my record, because the teacher didn't write me up. Usually, I got written up for every little thing—like cutting some guy with a pocket knife after gym class—and the dean was unreasonable. She told me to drop out and go get my G.E.D., like I was a dog." (The G.E.D. is the General Equivalency Diploma for high school.)

The other residents of the 104th Avenue group home didn't fare any better at Flushing. Like Crystal, they lacked educational skills, motivation, and discipline, felt overwhelmed by the size of the school, and fell through the cracks. St. Christopher's educational coordinator had a reason for sending them there. Among the common characteristics of students at Satellite Academy, a public city Alternative High School, with four campuses—two in Manhattan, one in the Bronx, and one in Jamaica, Queens—are that they have between ten and twenty credits and that they have attended ninth grade but have fallen behind their grade level; mostly students aged sixteen and older are accepted. To date, none of the group-home residents have stayed the course at Flushing, but going there at least exposed them to Langston Hughes and made them eligible to transfer to Satellite.

Satellite is a small, no-frills school, with a high faculty-to-student ratio. Its Jamaica campus has a hundred and ninety students, in the ninth, tenth, eleventh, and twelfth grades, and a staff of fourteen. About seventy percent of the students are black; most of the remainder are Hispanic. The school day is divided into six periods, or "slots," a day, and the school year is divided into four ten-week cycles. One of Satellite's purposes is to help students catch up. They are able to accumulate sixteen credits a year—four per cycle—rather than the ten per year they can accumulate in schools like Flushing. The six slots at the Jamaica campus don't include gym (there is no gymnasium), study hall (a frill), or calculus (few students spend more than two years at Satellite, and even those who do rarely manage to complete ninth- and tenth-grade math). Satellite's teachers consider the most important part of the curriculum to be Family Group, in which groups of between fifteen and eighteen students sit in a circle two or three times a week to discuss personal problems and school problems. For Family Group, the students are given credits in English. In the past, they were also given credits for holding part-time jobs and internships and for doing independent study.

Crystal preferred Satellite to Flushing. It was smaller, her teachers were more lenient and casual (students addressed them by their first names), her peers were more congenial—and it was easier to cheat. Students who had an English test in the first or second slot would give the test questions and answers to those scheduled to take the test in the third or sixth slot. Crystal wrote down the questions and answers on her hand, or on a piece of paper she slipped into her blouse sleeve, or underneath the desk, or under the "test-exam." Students caught cheating weren't necessarily dismissed; they were just given zeros. The teachers were there because they had chosen to work with adolescents who had known trouble. Crystal's counsellor, a Princeton graduate and former case-worker, would follow her to the girls' bathroom, where she often went to meet a friend from another class; he would knock on the door and encourage her to return to the classroom.

Crystal didn't do well at Satellite during her first year. She hadn't changed her ways: she was excessively absent, late, and high. In January of 1988, several days before her eighteenth birthday and the end of her first semester, she considered dropping out—almost fifty percent of Satellite's students fail to graduate—and spoke of settling for her G.E.D. Her counsellor at Satellite and her social worker at St. Christopher's prevailed upon her to stay in school.

Crystal's eyes—hazel if she is wearing her contact lenses, brown if she isn't—gleam with remembered joy when she looks back upon her eighteenth birthday. Diamond had appeared at the group home with a Gucci bag and a pair of Gucci boots, three silvery balloons printed with the words "Happy Birthday, I Love You," and a bouquet of flowers. "Everyone's face lit up with jealousy," Crystal says.

Federal and state laws require child-care agencies like St. Christopher-Ottilie to offer family-planning services to children twelve years of age and over. Since her entry into the group home, Crystal had been using birth-control pills. In August, 1987, she had a series of stomach aches she attributed to the pill. The doctor she had been seeing regularly was on vacation. Another doctor recommended that Crystal stop taking the pill to give her body a rest. In February, 1988, she discovered that she was pregnant—"I guess because we done it so much," she says. Crystal told Diamond she was going to have an abortion: since she had one child in foster care, it struck her as wrong to have a second child. Diamond had no children, but he accepted Crystal's decision. He gave her an enormous white stuffed bear for Valentine's Day. Several days later, she wrote the following note: "I Crystal Taylor, Resident of St. Christopher-Ottilie, is writting letter to confirm that after talking with my social worker . . . I know my options that I can make, but being that I'm not ready to care for another child and financially I can't care for another child, so I rather have an *Obortion*."

On March 1st, ten days after the abortion, Diamond Madison removed a gold-link bracelet from his arm, transferred it to Crystal's, and went to jail on Riker's Island. He had been arrested twice with large sums of money on him and no way to account for how he had come by the money honestly, and was given a six-month sentence. With time off for good behavior, he served four months. Between March and July, Crystal visited him faithfully the three days a week she was permitted to visit.

She missed only two days: she was with little Daquan on Easter weekend, and with big Daquan on Mother's Day weekend.

Almost from the day a child is placed in foster care, plans are made to discharge the child. The original plan drawn up for Crystal by St. Christopher's was "discharge to biological mother." When Crystal was fifteen, this was not considered a realistic goal, because of Florence's drug addiction, refusal to seek help, and enduring homelessness. Throughout 1985, monthly attempts made by Crystal's social worker to reach Florence were futile: she didn't answer letters sent to her last known address, on Findlay Avenue. The social worker knew that Crystal visited her mother in the Bronx, often in a park, and talked to her on the phone fairly regularly, but Florence preferred to keep those contacts informal. Whenever a social worker asked Florence for a phone number, Florence said that Crystal knew how to get hold of her. Cousin Hazel had no telephone, but a woman in her apartment building who babysat for Crystal's younger siblings did, and there was a telephone at the nursing home where Florence's current man, Clarence, worked as a janitor.

Crystal acknowledged that some of her meetings with her mother were frustrating, because Florence was often high or intoxicated. "My mother didn't recognize me until I got right into her face," she said after one Saturday visit. A child-care worker who saw Florence when she came to the group home for the first time, around Thanksgiving of 1985, remembers her as "a fat bag, unkempt, unwashed, and boisterous, who talked too much, laughed too much, and made the mistake of asking for a beer." She also remembers that Crystal, who was fastidious and was dressed "impeccable," seemed embarrassed by her mother's behavior and determined never to look like her or sink to that level. "And yet," the child-care worker adds, "there was an unshakable bond between them."

Soon after Crystal turned sixteen, Special Services for Children accepted a "change of permanency goal" proposed by St. Christopher's for Crystal: discharge to independent living. In the world of foster care, there are goals within goals within goals. For the next several years, the long-term-treatment goals for Crystal included graduating from high school, securing a full-time job, and making a home for her son. Crystal was highly goal-resistant. She appeared in no hurry to get through school. Her social worker discovered when she contacted Flushing High School in May of 1986 that Crystal had been absent thirty days and late thirty-six times since January. She had little interest in employment. She had enjoyed a summer youth job in 1987 as a hospital receptionist, but a social worker noted in March of 1988 that "the only effort Crystal made to finding a job was talking about finding a job." And she declined St. Christopher's many attempts to interest her in a mother-child program, in which she would live in a St. Christopher's house with other young mothers and their children, attend school (day care would be provided for the mothers during their school hours), and look after Daquan evenings and weekends, thereby acquiring the "parenting skills" that the agency felt she needed. Crystal insisted that she wasn't ready for this. It suited her to have little Daquan exactly where he was—at the Hargroves', where she could be an every-other-weekend mother, and do a minimum of Pampering, feeding, and bathing him.

"I've got no parently patience," Crystal acknowledges. She found it arduous to take Daquan on outings. "It was hard for me to carry him in one hand and his carriage and my pocketbook in the other," she says. "The baby was heavy, and so was the carriage." Crystal's vision of motherhood was buying Daquan expensive toys at Christmas and leather clothes (his first Easter suit, when he was six months, was custom-made), and taking him on annual or semiannual outings to the circus or to amusement parks with big Daquan, "so's when he grows up he'll remember he went with his mommy and daddy to Sesame Place." The status quo was also acceptable to Daquan Jefferson.

Margaret Hargrove was content as well. The Long children had not suited her. A foster parent has the right to ask an agency to remove a child on short notice. Regina Long was the first to go—"due to unresolvable disruptive behavior in the Hargrove home," according to St. Christopher-Ottilie's records—in the fall of 1985. Her brother and two sisters were freed for adoption by the Family Court in January of 1986, but one by one they left the Hargroves—to go to another relative, another foster parent, another agency. Rawanda was the last of the Long children to leave the Hargroves', at the end of 1987.

Before little Daquan came to the Hargroves', Margaret Hargrove had given up her job at the diner to devote herself full time to foster care. In 1985, as the Long teen-agers began to depart, she took in Frances Smart, six, and Donna Smart, seven, who were the third and fourth children of a drug-addicted mother; she would never take a chance on another teen-ager. (Her sister adopted three of Ms. Smart's children, and Margaret Hargrove adopted Frances and Donna in 1989, and subsequently had Ms. Smart's twelfth and thirteenth children in foster care.)

It was financially to Margaret Hargrove's advantage to maintain six children in residence. She receives what she calls an adequate "paycheck," which depends on the age of the child (foster parents receive more for six-to-eleven-year-olds than for infants-to-five-year-olds and still more for children twelve or over) and on ever-changing rates. In December of 1984, when two-month-old Daquan Drummond was presented to Alice Hargrove, St. Christopher's sent Alice's mother a stipend of $242 a month for him. The current rates for foster-home care in the New York metropolitan area range from $386 to $526 per month for healthy children. For "special" children (those with moderate physical and/or mental disabilities) and "exceptional" children (those with illnesses like AIDS or other extreme physical or mental handicaps), the rates are $845 and $1,281 per month, respectively. These stipends are tax-free. Each child also receives a clothing allowance set by the state and has his or her dental and medical care covered by Medicaid (at a cost of between three and four dollars a day). An agency's administrative costs add to the yearly sum required to keep youngsters in foster care. The Hargroves receive the same amount of money for the children they adopt, because it is state policy to subsidize adoptions of foster children with handicaps or special conditions, and those who are considered hard to place: those who have been in foster care in the same home for at least eighteen months; siblings; children who have been freed for adoption for at least six months; and minority children who are over the age of eight and white children over the age of ten.

Social workers called regularly at the Hargrove home, and, because St. Christopher's has a low turnover rate, Crystal and little Daquan had only a few social workers apiece over their years in foster care. The Hargroves' house was depicted in favorable terms: it was quiet, efficient, well run; children were playing; dinner was cooking; homework was being done. The only negative observation made was that Margaret Hargrove, who was called "very directive," had a better relationship with her younger foster children than with her older foster children, with whom there was "underlying tension." Little Daquan's care was exemplary. A plump, adorable child, he was the "little prince" of the family, sociable, bubbling, active—a "joyous child who makes people smile" and "receives constant love and attention from foster mother, her daughter, and three teenage foster children." (He was subsequently doted on by Frances and

Donna Smart.) Goals were set for him, too—not just drinking from a cup but also increasing his vocabulary. He met them and might have met the second one faster if everyone else in the household hadn't anticipated his needs, leaving him with little motivation to express himself verbally. A worker who saw Crystal at the Hargroves' observed that she was extremely warm and affectionate toward her son, and that he recognized Crystal as "mommy" and "understands he has two mommies."

After Crystal turned sixteen, and Daquan had been in foster care for more than a year, it was harder for St. Christopher's to justify keeping him in foster care with Crystal as the "discharge resource," because her own discharge was too far off. Consequently, the agency made an attempt to discharge him. He would go to live with his biological father, because Daquan Jefferson had a job and parents who expressed a willingness to help him care for his child; it would be stipulated that Daquan retain custody only until Crystal had completed high school, had an apartment, and had a job that would enable her to support her son.

A great deal of effort was expended in 1986 and 1987 on discharging little Daquan to his father, but no discharge took place. The records do not make absolutely clear why, but they do reveal that the discharge was not what Daquan Jefferson or Crystal Taylor or Margaret Hargrove wanted. Daquan was willing to take his son, but he asked Margaret Hargrove if she would care for him during the day on weekdays once he had custody, and said he would care for the boy, with his parents, on weekends. Margaret Hargrove at first consented to this plan, but St. Christopher's did not. Crystal opposed having her son go to live in the Bronx. She felt he was receiving better care at the Hargroves' than he would at the Jeffersons', and claimed that once Daquan had custody he would try to limit her access to her son: Daquan had remained "in love with" Crystal long after she went on to date other men. When Margaret Hargrove was threatened with the departure of little Daquan—who slept with the Hargroves in their bed, and who, alone among their foster children, was taken out of town for Alice's college graduation, and to Disney World—she told Daquan Jefferson he could no longer visit his son in her home on Saturdays and Sundays. She, too, felt that little Daquan was getting better care with her than he would get in the Bronx. In 1986, she spoke of adopting Crystal, as if that would enable her to adopt little Daquan. When big Daquan's father, Elmer Jefferson, died, in May, 1987, the discharge plan foundered. Children whose goal is to be discharged to a relative are usually kept in care for only two years. St. Christopher's went to court numerous times to request extensions of placement for little Daquan; the extensions were granted.

As soon as Diamond Madison was released from jail, in July of 1988, the romance resumed, but, except for the sex, things were never quite the same. Crystal had taken a part-time job as a cashier at a discount store in May, and insisted on paying for their first night back together, at the Capri. Diamond didn't immediately return to drug dealing—he knew that the cops who had arrested him twice would be watching him closely—and he had little money. Crystal didn't want him dealing drugs, and encouraged him to get a job, just as she had done four years earlier with Daquan Jefferson. Diamond got an honest job for three weeks and then quit: nine-to-five didn't suit his temperament. He eventually returned to selling drugs, but on a much smaller scale. When Crystal asked him for a suede skirt, he said she would have to wait, and bought himself sneakers instead. Her friends teased her. "Daquan would buy you anything," they said, "and still all you want is Diamond."

Not quite all. While Diamond was in jail, Crystal had hung out with two other drug dealers (including the one "I screwed for five minutes, first time I ever regretted that") and had started smoking coolies and "woolas" (a mixture of reefer and crack). Diamond sold crack but didn't use it. "He was afraid of me turning out to be a crackhead," Crystal says. "He told me to stay away from the guys I had been with while he was in jail. I said I would, but I didn't, and he beat me up outside the group home several times—1988 was my year of crack. I told Diamond about Kyle, the first guy I had intercourse with after he got out of jail, because I felt guilty. He then started fooling around with other girls, and I messed around with other guys, who could show me the good life."

That summer, the social worker Crystal had had for

two years left St. Christopher's. Her new social worker warned her that unless she showed the court that she was making progress toward achieving her goals she would eventually lose custody of her child to Daquan. Daquan had never threatened anything of the kind, but after nearly four years in the group home Crystal was ready to get on with her life for reasons of her own. The dealers who provided her with drugs hung out on Hempstead Avenue, a few blocks from the group home, where there was a cluster of small shops—bodegas, a Chinese carryout, a video store. At first, they supplied her with complimentary crack. Soon she had to buy her own, and she decided that it wasn't a good investment: the money would be better spent on clothes. She wanted to put some distance between herself and temptation.

By 1988, the five girls who had celebrated Crystal's fifteenth birthday with her were long gone. Lynn had left at the age of eighteen, in the summer of 1985, after graduating from Satellite, because she was sick of being in foster care; she went to live with a boyfriend and had a child two years later. Tina and Simone left for similar reasons, and also had babies. Yolanda turned to crack. Nicole became a prostitute. Fifteen or twenty other girls had entered and left 104th Avenue between 1985 and 1988. A roommate of Crystal's—one of the two with whom she travelled to the movies on Forty-second Street instead of to Flushing High—had a psychotic episode, smashed a number of mirrors and windows at the group home, and wound up in a psychiatric hospital. A few girls went to live with relatives. Two or three went to college. Some were forced to leave, because they refused to go to school. Several simply left: one day they were there, the next day they weren't. They were never seen again. The staff learned what had happened to one former resident only when they read about her in a newspaper: she had been arrested for transporting guns from the South to New York City by Greyhound bus.

Crystal's favorite period at the group home was her first six months. "We used to always sit down and have conversations about things like sex," she recalls. "What a man expects from a woman, how he treats a woman after having sex, me and the other girls, each one voicing they opinions. I was the youngest, so I was getting more of a learning. I was getting wiser." She has referred to a couple of her original housemates as "the older sisters I never had" and to several of the staff members as "family." After those six months, Crystal began to complain about how much her housemates stole from her. Stealing is commonplace in congregate living, and Crystal flaunted her leather coats and bags and gold jewelry—gifts from Daquan, Diamond, and her other male acquaintances. She complained about the constant thefts but never gave her valuables to the child-care workers for safekeeping. With each passing year, she displayed more reluctance to do her chores, to refrain from using profanity, to obey her curfew. She bribed one child-care worker with beer when she returned late from dates. She seemed to know just how many hours she could be AWOL and how much drinking and drugs she could do without getting tossed out. It was as if she had made up her mind to stay at the group home as long as possible, because she knew of no better alternative. She was the only one to come to 104th Avenue after having a child; she had been where the others were going.

In 1985, six former foster-care recipients between the ages of eighteen and twenty-one who had been discharged to independent living and three recipients currently in group homes who expected to be discharged brought suit against the governor of New York, claiming lack of supervision of those discharged and lack of provision of discharge plans or transition services before discharge for the others. The primary reason for the lawsuit seemed to be that a substantial number of people in homeless shelters had been discharged from foster care. The case resulted in greater attention to preparing older children to live independently upon discharge from foster care and to arranging more orderly discharges. Agencies like St. Christopher-Ottilie had been providing many such transition services but had not been adequately funded for them until the suit was settled, in 1986.

Crystal was fortunate. St. Christopher's opened an independent-living apartment for two girls in 1987 and a second in 1988. In October of 1988, Crystal applied for admission to an independent-living apartment. The first tenants of the 1987 apartment had recently been evicted for breaking one of the cardinal independent-living-apartment rules: no overnight guests. During Crystal's second year at Satellite, her attendance improved. Students had to sign a contract with each teacher, agreeing to a maximum number of cuts per subject in a cycle; if they exceeded the cuts, they were not given credit for the subject even if they attained a passing grade. In the fall of 1988, Crystal took night classes at Jamaica High School in two subjects she had failed the previous year at Satellite—math and English. It seemed that she would be able to graduate in June, 1989, and that presumption was a point in her favor when she was being considered for an independent-living apartment. The staff at the group home had always been fond of Crystal—her keen sense of humor and her lack of self-pity were endearing qualities that made many adults forgive her temper tantrums, outbursts of obscenity, and selfishness—but as she grew older and became a house leader they worried about the poor example she set the younger girls, and thought she should move on. On December 27, 1988, Crystal moved into the independent-living apartment that had been opened the previous year. Her roommate was Benita, an alumna of another St. Christopher's group home.

The apartment, which was situated in Jamaica, a twenty-minute ride from the 104th Avenue group home, in Queens Village, occupied the second floor of a two-family house. It had a separate entrance on the ground floor and its own staircase. The bedroom was sufficiently large to accommodate twin beds and two dressers; the living room, kitchen, and bathroom were adequate; all the rooms had windows.

Crystal and Benita broke the rules of the independent-living apartment at once. Their girlfriends and boyfriends spent the night. No drugs or liquor were allowed on the premises. They drank Absolut vodka and Rémy-Martin cognac, kept a six-pack of wine coolers in the refrigerator, and smoked reefer. Shortly after moving in, however, Crystal did give up crack. When they had been in the apartment a few months, a social worker paid an unscheduled visit, and saw a "roach" (marijuana butt) in an ashtray. Crystal and Benita lied their way out of the situation by saying that a girlfriend had come over and smoked reefer; they claimed they had told her to put it out and she had, but they hadn't dumped the ashtray. The social worker's advice was that if they couldn't keep their company from doing drugs in the apartment they shouldn't have company. "They bought our story and threatened us with more pop-up visits, but they didn't follow through for a long time," Crystal says.

One way an independent-living apartment helped young women make the transition from group-home life to life on their own was by enabling them to save money. Their rent and all utilities were paid, and they had access to a revolving cash fund of up to two hundred and twenty-five dollars a week. That sum was intended to cover groceries, cleaning supplies, laundry, dry cleaning, transportation to school and work, and such recreational activities as movies. To be reimbursed for their legitimate expenses, all they had to do was to produce receipts for the money they had spent. They were also given a clothing allowance and an additional monthly stipend from the state of between twenty and forty dollars a month (twenty dollars at age sixteen, forty at age twenty). The independent-living residents who were employed full time or part time were supposed to show their social workers their paychecks and bank books: they were expected to bank half of their earnings and also the stipends. Their savings—some girls left the agency with two or three thousand dollars—might be spent on a month's security deposit and the first month's rent on an apartment after they left the St. Christopher's apartment.

Crystal had injured her thumb operating the cash register at her job in the spring of 1988, and had quit during the summer. Her new social worker urged her to get another job. In February of 1989, she found an after-school job at Cheap John's, a store that featured bargain goods. ("Five rolls of toilet paper for a dollar," Crystal recalls.)

A week or two after she started there, she found more lucrative employment when Furman, a Jamaican with short dreadlocks who supplied Crystal with weed and tried unsuccessfully to date her, offered her five hundred dollars plus expenses to carry half a pound of cocaine to Washington, D.C. All the other girls he had used as couriers had been caught. Furman said he would accompany her on the first run, on February 21st, to show her what to do. The twenty-first was a Tuesday, so Crystal went to Satellite, to her four-to-eight job at Cheap John's, and to Furman's house to fetch the goods. Following his instructions, she wrapped a Ziploc bag of cocaine in a paper bag, put the paper bag at the bottom of a large Gucci pocketbook she used as a book bag, and covered it with books. They took a cab to Thirty-sixth Street and walked to Penn Station—Crystal walking a few steps behind Furman. He had given her a hundred and fifty dollars and some instructions: if he was picked up on the train, she was to take a train back home. He had given her enough money for the return trip. Crystal bought a one-way ticket. They left New York on an evening train. They sat on opposite sides of the aisle, acting like strangers. Crystal looked at one of her schoolbooks, did a little homework, and then read a novel by Jackie Collins, her favorite author. They arrived at Washington's Union Station after midnight. Furman got into a cab, looked around, and told her to jump in: his fear of getting caught appeared to be over. They travelled a short distance to a four-story building. Two men were waiting for them in a small apartment. While the men busied themselves at the kitchen stove, turning the cocaine into crack, Crystal stayed in a bedroom, watching television. Furman handed her a hundred dollars for a shuttle ticket home and the five hundred dollars she had earned. Crystal had been nervous on the train. That night she slept on and off, but she realized that what she was doing was dangerous; she felt afraid, and prayed that the night would end and the daylight would come. In the morning, Furman took her to a McDonald's for breakfast and then drove her, in a car that belonged to one of the Washington drug dealers, to National Airport. Crystal used her Satellite identification to buy a shuttle ticket at the student rate. It was the first time she had flown, and she liked it: flying was exciting. She took a cab from LaGuardia to the independent-living apartment and tossed about six hundred dollars in tens and twenties on the coffee table—her earnings, plus the extra train and plane money. She called Tonia at the group home.

"Where have you been?" Tonia asked her. "Diamond's been going crazy looking for you. Benita called me to ask where you was. He was in the apartment all night with her. He thought Benita knew you was sleeping with another man and just wasn't saying anything. At first, he wouldn't let Benita go to school, but then he did. You better get your lies together, because your Diamond is mad, he's really mad."

Crystal asked Tonia to come over to the apartment, by cab, at Crystal's expense, to keep her company: she was afraid of Diamond. Crystal went into the bathroom and took a shower. She heard the doorbell, put on a T-shirt, and went downstairs to answer it with a big grin: she was thinking about spending the money. It was Diamond. "Where you was?" he asked.

Crystal stuttered and hesitated, then turned and walked up the stairs.

"Come here," he said, standing in the living room as she headed for the bedroom to put on some clothes. He saw the cash on the coffee table. "Where did you get this money?" he asked. "You slept with a man for money. I know you."

Crystal told him she had earned the money carrying cocaine to Washington. She was happy she had made the drop safely and happy he'd been worried about her. In retrospect, Crystal thinks she smiled a little too hard. Diamond hit her. She hit him back. She tried to punch him as hard as he punched her. Then Tonia pulled up in a cab, and a friend of Diamond's also came upstairs. They couldn't break up the fight. Diamond knocked the cap off Crystal's front tooth. He thought he had really hurt her and tried to hug her. Crystal wanted to fight him some more. "I'm getting out of here, you fucking crazy," Diamond said when she hit him again. He snatched two hundred dollars of the money from the table and left. She thought he was trying to take temporary custody of all the money, to show her that what she had done was wrong, and grabbed the rest of the cash. When Crystal later spoke to Precious, another girlfriend of hers whom Diamond had called, she reprimanded Crystal for not having told Diamond she was going to Mrs. Hargrove's for the night—an alibi that would have covered her.

"I didn't carry no more drugs for Furman," Crystal says. "Even if Diamond hadn't hit me—and when he found out who I did it for he gave me another argument—I wouldn't have did it again. Diamond dealt in drugs, but he said he was a man what could take care of hisself. He reminded me I could have gotten killed in that apartment and that I had a son. He loved little Daquan. It was easy money, but it was too scary and I was afraid of losing Diamond's respect for good. I loved that man so much until it hurted." Crystal sought refuge in the group home on the night of the eighth.

When the staff of St. Christopher's learned that Crystal had been in a physical fight, her apartment was searched and her plane ticket found. "I told the social worker some nonsense about my girlfriend's boyfriend getting shot up in Virginia and she had no one to go with her and she'd pay for my ticket and I'd gone down there—some lame story," she says. "They suspected I'd done something illegal, but they didn't know what. I'd broken a rule, because I wasn't allowed to leave the state. I told them Diamond had hit me because I hadn't told him where I was going. They acted like they believed that, because he'd hit me hard before." The agency nurse referred Crystal to a dentist, and she got the cap put back on her tooth.

Crystal did not return to Cheap John's: "I was tired of seeing them same old dull faces." In March, she got a temporary afternoon job in a vast room on West Fourteenth Street, in Manhattan, stuffing and sealing envelopes. Four weeks later, a layoff notice was posted near the time cards. That same week, Crystal heard from Veronica, a girl with whom she had drunk rum-and-Coca-Cola at J.H.S. 109. Veronica was working in the mailroom at an advertising agency on Madison Avenue at Fiftieth Street, and said the firm was hiring. Crystal had always liked the idea of "working with the big rich people in the big Manhattan buildings." On a rainy day, after picking up her last paycheck on Fourteenth Street, Crystal walked around the East Fifties and filled out applications at several firms in the area's glassy skyscrapers. A month later, she received a call from the advertising agency and went for a job interview. Crystal had already forgotten the job application, and Veronica had quit because one of the outside messengers who came up to the mailroom was pestering her. Crystal was hired as a part-time mail clerk. Her hours—4:30 P.M. to 9 P.M.—enabled her to continue at Satellite, which ended its day at 3 P.M.

Her first day of work was May 1st. The pay was four dollars and twenty-five cents an hour, not even a dollar above the minimum wage, but the job had an appealing fringe benefit: the company sent employees who stayed at work after 8 P.M. home by car service. That saved two homeward-bound subway and bus tokens per day—ten dollars' worth of tokens a week, in 1989—and an hour's travel time. Crystal, who already had her learner's permit, had always preferred cars to mass transit. In June, although she still needed to complete two courses before she could get her diploma, she participated in graduation ceremonies at Satellite, in a white cap and gown. Big Daquan rented a car for her in honor of the occasion (he has never had a driver's license or owned wheels of any kind, so Crystal did the driving), and little Daquan and Diamond attended the graduation. Crystal dropped out of summer school ("I couldn't deal with it in the nice weather"), finished her coursework at

Satellite in the fall, and picked up her diploma in January of 1990, shortly after her twentieth birthday. By then, she was working full time at the ad agency, from 2 to 9 P.M. By then, little Daquan was living in the Bronx and was halfway through kindergarten.

Crystal and Daquan had been presented with an ultimatum in the fall of 1988: Take little Daquan out of foster care or give him up for adoption. No further extensions of placement would be considered; more people are willing to adopt babies and small children than to adopt older ones, so adoption becomes the permanency plan if return to the family is not possible or advisable. Foster parents are usually given the first chance to adopt children who have been in their care. Margaret Hargrove proposed an "open adoption" to Crystal and Daquan, in which the biological parents would retain certain rights of access, but although neither of them wanted to have their son on a full-time basis, neither of them had any intention of forfeiting any parental rights. Daquan Jefferson agreed to take his son until Crystal was out of foster care herself and was financially on her feet. Margaret Hargrove had other small children in foster care in 1989, but little Daquan was still her favorite. When he went to the Bronx for pre-discharge trial weekends at the Jeffersons', she expressed her displeasure over his imminent departure. She told her social worker that little Daquan was not supervised properly during the weekend visits, and returned to "the foster home in an obstinate manner." She also reported his reaction to her social worker: "This is my house and you're going to put me out of my goddam house," he had said. "The Bronx is dirty." Little Daquan moved to the Jeffersons' in September, 1989.

"One reason Daquan wanted the baby was he knew he'd see me more," Crystal says, and he did: she visited every weekend or two. Margaret Hargrove gave little Daquan a party for his fifth birthday—she invited his parents and other members of Crystal's family—and telephoned the Jefferson household frequently throughout the following months.

For his fifth birthday, Crystal gave her son a two-hundred-and-fifty-dollar gold bracelet with his name in diamonds. It was one of the rare moments after Diamond's release from jail when he had money to spare, and he contributed a hundred dollars toward the bracelet. Around that time, he asked Crystal for a hundred and fifty dollars, so that he could go job-hunting. She took the money out of her bank account. He spent it, along with money borrowed from other friends, on a secondhand Kawasaki Ninja motorcycle. Crystal was not pleased. Diamond and a friend made some money hauling dirt to construction sites with a dump truck and sold a little crack, but he wouldn't get an honest job and earn real money. "You started off doing for me. How are you going to end it like this?" Crystal asked him. Diamond came every now and again to what Crystal referred to as "the independent house" or invited her to his mother's apartment. After they had been in bed an hour or two, one of his friends inevitably paged him on a beeper and he left in a hurry. "His friends said 'Jump' and he answered 'How high?' " Crystal recalls. "He put them in front of me to hang out. I always said they would be the death of him."

By 1990, Crystal had a beeper herself, and was hanging out with an assortment of young drug dealers. They kept her in reefer and had plenty of money to buy her a pair of sneakers or a leather jacket and to take her to restaurants, parties, and clubs. She liked being wined and dined and riding around in their jeeps, BMWs, and "Benzes." She was having fun.

Her social worker was not pleased. The original plan for the independent-living apartments was that they were to be used by the residents for a year and a half at the most. The social worker wanted to "trial-discharge" Crystal in the summer of 1990, so that if she ran into trouble afterward St. Christopher's could again help her—though only for six months, until she reached twenty-one, the day the money stopped. In the spring of 1990, Crystal ducked many of her required weekly appointments with the social worker, didn't see the St. Christopher's psychologist (although he was one of her favorite people at the agency), and let her bank account dwindle. She was buying clothes and jewelry, having acrylic tips put on her nails, and getting her hair done. (When she was a little girl on Sheridan Avenue, her favorite possession was a doll whose hair she could wash, braid, curl on small rollers, and blow-dry. She played with it for hours; it was one way to tune out the misery that sur-

[75]

rounded her.) Crystal has a talent for hair, and her hair style changes frequently—from a simple set with bangs to a French twist, or perhaps to a very elaborate affair, requiring the addition of blond braids or a hairpiece woven with seed pearls. Crystal had grown weary of group-home discussions and now ducked various obligatory independent-living-unit meetings, sensitivity groups, and workshops. They took time from her men and from her job. She particularly objected to an independent-living workshop held upstate, which caused her to miss four days at the office.

"She basically uses the independent-living-apartment program as a boarding house," her social worker wrote on her record. "She enjoys all the benefits but is reluctant to put anything back into it. . . . She makes little effort to help with responsibilities connected to the program, i.e. money management, dropping off receipts, attending workshops, and keeping appointments." Crystal felt that her part of the independent-living bargain consisted simply of working at the ad agency.

Crystal mentioned to the social worker that she was having trouble with her boss about her hours of employment: she preferred daytime hours. The social worker offered to help her seek another job, but her schedule was soon switched; for a time it was 9 A.M. to 5 P.M., and then 6:30 A.M. to 2:30 P.M. She dallied about seeking an apartment. She admitted that she was afraid of letting go. She wanted to age out of St. Christopher's at twenty-one. She was lucky to live in one of the few states in the United States that keep young people in care until that age. In April, the social worker drove her to the Y.W.C.A. in Brooklyn. While she was there, a young man called on a woman resident, and the young woman had to come downstairs to see him. "I ain't living where nobody can't visit my room, in nobody's Y, in nobody's Brooklyn," Crystal said, and did not pursue residence at the Y.

While Crystal's social worker was planning Crystal's discharge, Crystal and Daquan were unplanning little Daquan's. In June, 1990, little Daquan, wearing a lime-green cap and gown, received a diploma from a Catholic kindergarten in the Bronx, in which his father had enrolled him. When Florence was evicted from the apartment on Sheridan Avenue, back in 1982, her furniture and other possessions had been confiscated by the marshals. She hadn't retrieved them. Most of Crystal's childhood photographs were lost, to her regret, so she tends to take photographs of the joyful events in her life. In the snapshots of her son's graduation, Crystal has on a three-piece peach-colored pants outfit that shows her trim figure to advantage. The outfit had a three-hundred-dollar price tag, but Daquan had bought it "hot" for fifty dollars from a friend who boosted clothes.

A week after his graduation, little Daquan was back at the Hargroves'. He was glad—there were no children his age at the Jeffersons', and he preferred playing with other youngsters in a back yard. So was his father—he liked to spend his time off from work with his friends. So was his mother—Crystal had never stopped believing that her son received better care on Long Island than he did in an increasingly dangerous part of the

Bronx among teen-agers and adults who had no interest in a child. Margaret Hargrove was overjoyed at the return of her "star" (as one social worker had described little Daquan). Daquan Jefferson agreed to pay his son's first-grade tuition at a Catholic school on Long Island and to pay for school uniforms, and contributed fifty dollars every now and then for the child's clothes. Margaret Hargrove didn't ask for money for food, and spent additional money to clothe little Daquan to her satisfaction. She had no trouble hiding him from the social worker who called on her regularly to see the six other children living in her home, for whom she was certified.

A week after her son's return to Long Island, Crystal took up with a young Jamaican drug dealer named Troy, who was tall and husky and always wore dress pants, a silk shirt, and leather shoes—"like he was going somewhere," Crystal recalls. "Like he had a job on Wall Street. But no tie." She told all her friends she still hoped that Diamond would get a job and that someday they would be together, but added that she liked Troy better than the other men with whom she had been consorting. He was muscular, and he was tall: he reminded her of Diamond.

On Monday evening, July 23, 1990, the phone rang at the independent-living apartment. Crystal was in the shower—she had just come in from jogging with Troy—and threw a towel around herself and answered the phone. It was a friend of Benita's. She asked Crystal if she was sitting down, and said she had some bad news for her. While Crystal was thinking that this girl never called *her*, and was wondering what kind of bad news she could possibly have, and was trying to get her off the phone—she had to get dressed—Benita's friend told her that Diamond was dead. "Stop playing with me," Crystal said. Her voice started to crack when the girl told her where his death had occurred—at the intersection of Hempstead Avenue and Springfield Boulevard, not far from 104th Avenue. Crystal hung up, and called the group home, thinking that the child-care worker on duty would know if anything had happened to Diamond. The worker had heard nothing. Crystal and a friend took a cab to Hempstead and Springfield. A group of people, including one of Diamond's close friends, were standing outside a restaurant there. After painting the Ninja that morning, Diamond had gone to the restaurant that afternoon to buy his grandmother some food. As he was standing on the corner drinking a soda, eating chips, and talking to a drug dealer whom Crystal knew only as Duke, a man in a blue Mazda, who had quarrelled with Duke, pulled up and, while waiting at a stoplight outside the restaurant, sprayed bullets at both men. Duke was wounded. Diamond was killed.

When Crystal's social worker went to the apartment the next day, Crystal was distraught. She spoke of all the good times she had had with Diamond. When she was at the group home on Christmas Eve, she recalled, he had interrupted his drug dealing at eleven-fifty-nine to wish her a Merry Christmas, and he had done the same a week later, to wish her a Happy New

Year. Even after they had split up, he went out to the Hargroves' by himself to see little Daquan. "I seen a future with him," Crystal said. The social worker held her, comforted her, and drove her to Diamond's mother's house so that she could pay her respects. The social worker also spent time with Crystal the following day. Crystal hadn't gone to work on Monday: Troy had rented a car for her, so that she could drive her girlfriends to a concert at Giants Stadium on Sunday. She and Troy had returned the car on Monday, then had brunch at a diner and made love at the house he had bought for his mother, near the independent-living house. She took the rest of the week off to attend Diamond's wake and funeral. Troy accompanied her to a store and chose and paid for a black-and-white hat for the funeral. She had told Troy about Diamond's taking her hundred and fifty dollars and spending it on a bike. "This is what happens to people who do wrong to you," Troy had said.

In September, Crystal reluctantly returned to the process of apartment hunting. She was reading the real-estate ads, as her social worker had taught her, and she observed that most of the listings were asking for "principals only." She asked the social worker why landlords wanted to rent only to school officials. The social worker explained that "principals only" meant "of urgent importance." (In a real-estate ad, "principals only" actually means that only the person who intends to rent the apartment—not an agent seeking to list it—should respond to the ad.) Crystal was amused by her own mistake. She apartment-hunted halfheartedly.

On Sunday, November 4, 1990, Crystal beeped Troy. She was with Charissa, a girl who lived diagonally across the street from the independent-living apartment. Charissa was friendly with one of Troy's brothers, and on the previous June 15th she had invited Crystal to Troy's birthday party; that was when Crystal had met and started dating him. Troy always behaved toward Crystal in what she felt was a considerate manner. He invited her "to be his company" when he drove his mother from Jamaica to a beauty salon in Brooklyn where she chose to have her hair done, and when he drove to downtown Brooklyn to buy fish for the barbecues held at his house. He took her to the movies after work, once taking along his daughter (who lived with him) and little Daquan, and he drove her out to the Hargroves' to return Daquan after a weekend visit. He gave her a hundred dollars for a leather jacket for little Daquan, asked what she wanted him to bring her from his trips to Florida, and spent most evenings with her: they went to restaurants and clubs, and went on a party-boat ride.

Troy, driving a jeep, pulled up in front of the independent-living apartment around six o'clock. Crystal was still standing outside Charissa's house. Another jeep pulled up in front of Troy's, and two young men got out. As Crystal crossed the street, she saw that one of the men was walking on

Susan Sheehan

the sidewalk toward her house. The other was walking in the
same direction out in the street. His eyes met hers as they
both approached the jeep. She said hello to Troy. The man
walked past her, then turned around and, having apparently
satisfied himself that the track was clear, pulled out a gun. As
Crystal backed off, toward Charissa's, Troy and the gunman
exchanged words. She heard a shot. The two men drove away.
Troy tried to get out of his jeep but couldn't, managed to put
it in gear, and drove it into a tree. Some men came out of
nearby houses and tried to extricate him from the jeep. Crystal, in a panic, ran to Troy's house to find one of his brothers.
By the time they got back to the scene of the shooting, police
and an ambulance were there. Troy was still talking when the
police arrived. By the time Crystal got to the hospital where
he had been taken, he was dead. The police asked her to go to
a nearby precinct and questioned her. She told them what she
had seen. The next thing she remembers is waking up, heavily
sedated, in a hospital in Queens. On Monday, two staff members from St. Christopher's picked her up at the hospital and
drove her to the 104th Avenue group home. They were upset
that she had been overmedicated and that she was being
treated like a criminal. Crystal was still groggy and distraught
on Tuesday. In the child-care worker's bedroom, she and
Benita and Charissa talked about avenging Troy's death. On
Wednesday, Crystal left the group home with Charissa. They
bought a wig for Crystal to wear, so that she wouldn't be

recognized by Troy's killers, if they were in the neighborhood, and went on to Troy's house.

"They saying you got Troy killed," Troy's brother Tony told her.

"Who saying that?" she asked.

"Troy's wife. You knew he was married, didn't you?"

"Excuse me. Troy was married?"

Crystal had no idea that Troy had a wife and two daughters, living in another house he owned. Her mood changed from grief to anger. "I felt dissed and cheated," she says. "Troy never gave me any suspicions he was married and had two daughters other than the one what lived with him, because he always beeped me right back, we spent a night in his room at his mother's house, and he showed me off in front of all his friends. We were supposed to go to Jamaica together before Christmas. I didn't tell him I was living in an apartment paid for by the government, and I ain't ask him what he did when I wasn't with him."

Crystal, wearing the wig, went to Troy's wake early on Friday morning, before either the killers or members of the family were likely to be there. She had spent the night with Lonnie, a nineteen-year-old drug dealer who had been in prison. After Lonnie got out of prison, at the end of the summer, she had smoked reefer and had sex with him when she wasn't with Troy. Her fling with Lonnie was brief. "He acted childish, and I wasn't into babysitting," she says. If Charissa hadn't been present when

Crystal learned that Troy was married, Crystal would have kept the news to herself, to avoid losing face with her wide circle of friends. On Monday, she went back to work.

Crystal's social workers had known for years about her involvement with drug dealers, and had taken note of the expensive gifts they gave her. She had more gold jewelry than any of the other girls in the group home, and wore chains with a big Nefertiti pendant, a Nefertiti ring, half a dozen other chains and rings, and large gold shell earrings. Though many items were stolen from her at the group home and in two unsolved burglaries at the independent-living apartment, in which she lost not only much of her jewelry but also her son's name bracelet, there was always someone new to replace the valuables. The deaths of Diamond and Troy within three and a half months made the agency nervous. Perhaps Crystal wasn't dealing drugs, but she was associating with drug dealers, and the shots were getting too close. It was time for her to leave St. Christopher's. When Crystal's social worker paid a surprise visit to her apartment in November and found roaches in the ashtrays and wine coolers in the refrigerator, Crystal was told to find an apartment of her own immediately.

On December 5, 1990, Crystal Taylor moved out of the independent-living apartment and into a studio apartment in the basement of a one-family house in Hollis, Queens, fifteen minutes away by car. She had been in St. Christopher's care for five years and eleven months. Her first post-foster-care apartment was small, dark, and drearily furnished. She had found it by buying a newspaper—Crystal has virtually no interest in the news and very rarely buys a paper—and scanning the real-estate ads. Lonnie had driven her around to look at apartments. The rent was five hundred and twenty-five dollars a month. The double bed sagged and smelled of mildew; water, not light, seeped into the place.

Crystal received a hundred-dollar discharge grant for clothing and a five-hundred-dollar discharge grant for furniture. She spent the five hundred dollars on a new double bed. She left St. Christopher's angry—she felt she had been hurried out instead of being allowed to stay until her twenty-first birthday, and she didn't like having to wait for her discharge grants until she produced receipts for her purchases—but she was also grateful. "If I hadn't been put in foster care, I'd have gone back to the Jeffersons'," she says. "Without the agency pushing me and keeping me thinking right, I'd have been a junior-high-school dropout. Me and Daquan would have had a couple of more kids before breaking up. I'd have stayed on drugs, and I'd probably be on welfare. I wouldn't be working for an advertising agency. I'd never have met Diamond. The staffs at St. Christopher's told me that if I had been fourteen in 1990 me and little Daquan would have gone home to the Jeffersons'. They say the system is getting more overloaded. My timing was right. Things happen for a reason. St. Christopher's gave me a second chance at life."

Crystal enjoyed smoking reefer, drinking liquor, and entertaining her male companions in her new apartment, without social workers arriving unannounced and pointing out how many agency rules she had broken, but by January 1st she missed St. Christopher's subsidies. She had previously been able to spend her take-home pay—about three hundred and twenty dollars every two weeks, without overtime—on additions to her stylish wardrobe. In the fall of 1990, she had cheerfully gone shopping after work, buying silk blouses, pricing Louis Vuitton wallets, putting leather jackets on layaway. After December, her earnings scarcely covered her rent, her phone bill, and her beeper bill. "I'm not shopping, that's the sadness in my life," she observed to a friend. "There's nothing like having something else."

On January 15th, Crystal received an upsetting piece of news. Little Daquan had told his teacher that Mrs. Hargrove hit him in the face with a stick. Crystal had visited her son regularly while he was in the Bronx but had slacked off after his return to the Hargroves', because she knew he was safe there, and because she was too busy running around with Troy and Jimbo and Star—other drug dealers she was seeing. Daquan Jefferson had not been visiting his son much, either. Crystal knew that Mrs. Hargrove might "chastise" Daquan but would never hit him. Since Mrs. Hargrove had all the foster children and adopted children she was certified to have, she felt she could not jeopardize her situation as a foster parent, so she told Crystal to please fetch little Daquan in three days. Crystal believed that her son's lie was his way of getting his parents to pay some attention to him. In January of 1991, Daquan, six, went back to the Bronx to live with his father, his grandmother, and his teen-age cousins—the children of one of Daquan's brothers, who had used drugs and died of pneumonia.

In January, a week after her birthday, Crystal was introduced to Tarrant, a thirty-nine-year-old Bahamian who owned a grocery store in the Canarsie section of Brooklyn, by an acquaintance who had once worked part time for him, off the books. Tarrant was busy in his store Mondays through Saturdays from about 10 A.M. to 2 or 3 A.M. and netted about a thousand dollars a week. He sold everything—bread and condoms, cigarettes and beer, milk and envelopes (three cents apiece). He smoked reefer, but he didn't drink much and didn't sell drugs. "He was too scared," Crystal says. She wasn't taken by his looks. He had plain features and "he always needed a decent haircut and a shave." His clothes were custom-made but unstylish; to Crystal it seemed that he could be mistaken for "a bum on a train." She was attracted to Tarrant by what his money could buy her. He gave her a VCR two weeks after they met, as a belated twenty-first-birthday present. He bought her a heater for her dank apartment, gave her a hundred dollars here and two hundred dollars there to have her hair done, to buy a dress, to pay some of her bills. He gave her groceries.

Crystal was not physically attracted to Tarrant, and for a few weeks she fended him off by saying she wasn't sexually active. When she finally had to go to bed with him, she got herself "really cheebered up" on marijuana beforehand. She knew she had to spend Sundays with him, when the store was closed, and although he was considerate—on his birthday, he took her to City Island to eat lobster, her favorite food—Crystal found him boring. He asked too many questions about things that she thought were self-evident. He called her at ten-thirty one night to ask her what she was doing. She said, "Getting ready to go to sleep. What the fuck do you think I'm doing? I have to be up at 4:30 A.M. to get ready for work." Tarrant bored Crystal more after he was robbed at gunpoint in his store one night in May. He lost about thirty-five hundred dollars and had less money to spend on her. When he didn't give her a television set that he had promised her as a Mother's Day present, she told him, "Mother's Day comes just once a year." When he answered, "I'm backed up on my bills," she said, "That sounds personal. I don't got nothing to do with that. Just give me mine." She did entertain a few doubts about using him. "If you go to bed with a man for money and not pleasure, it's not good for the other part of you," she says. Crystal got the TV set from Tarrant and started dating Stanley, a young man who had no money but was more fun to be with—for a while. Then she started seeing Glenn, a young man who sold drugs on her block, where one house stood out for what it was—a crack house, to and from which dealers roared in their cars and on motorcycles day and night.

In July of 1991, Crystal contemplated a relaxing summer. Little Daquan was going to Savannah, Georgia, to stay with some of his father's relatives from early July until mid-August; she wouldn't have to make the trek to the Bronx for six weeks. Tarrant was going home to Nassau to visit his family for the first two weeks of August. She would be free to watch her twenty-five-inch Sharp TV with stereo, and be cooled by a fan Tarrant had recently provided, with Herb, a van driver she had met while riding with him as a passenger, or with Cyril, a subway-maintenance man she had met at a subway station, or with Glenn, who had "put some zest back in my life."

Before Tarrant flew to Nassau, on August 1st, he gave Crystal five hundred and seventy-five dollars. Some of it was designated for little Daquan's return train fare from Savannah and some for her telephone and credit-card bills. Tarrant had also told Crystal to use some of the money for a deposit at the Jack La Lanne Health Spa near her office (she wanted to improve her stomach muscles), and said that after his return he would give her the money for the monthly fee. While Tarrant was away, she went to Jack La Lanne twice after work. She got more exercise in bed. Over Friday and Saturday one week, she had to change her satin sheets (another gift from Tarrant) twice. By the time Tarrant returned, she was through with Cyril ("He treated me like a common slut") and Herb ("He was too childish") and was angry with Glenn, who had dropped out of sight a few days earlier.

By late August, Crystal was neglecting Tarrant for Marcel, an outside messenger she had met at work. "I never really knew what to say to Tarrant," she says. "Marcel had no money, but I could be myself with him. We'd walk down Lexington Avenue and I'd laugh so hard the bones in my cheeks used to hurt, and he'd be laughing, too."

On Sunday, September 8, 1991, at about 3 A.M., Crystal returned to Queens from the Bronx, where she had been shopping for school clothes for little Daquan and hanging out in a park with Marcel. As she and Marcel approached her apartment, she spotted Tarrant's van parked outside and told Marcel to turn around and go back up the block. Tarrant didn't see him, but he started to argue with her. She told him she was going into the house. He got out of the van and stormed into the apartment behind her. She took her sneakers off, and he kept arguing with her. "I'm getting out of here," she said, and bent down to put her sneakers back on. "You ain't leaving out of here," Tarrant said. "You don't love me, and I don't have nothing to live for right now. I might as well take you and me together." As she was putting on her second sneaker, she heard four clicks.

She looked up and saw a 9-mm. pistol pointed at her head. It had malfunctioned. Tarrant set the gun down on the table, quickly pulled a smaller pistol out of his pocket—a .22-calibre —and aimed it at her head. Before he pulled the trigger, Crystal put her left hand up to her head—a reflex action. The smaller pistol was working—Crystal heard a loud *pow* and felt something strike her left hand. Tarrant got ready to pull the trigger again. Crystal grabbed him and cried, "Please don't, please don't!" He told her, "I got to kill you, because I shot you and you'll tell the police," and he kept the gun pointed at her.

Crystal apologized for having hurt Tarrant—she hadn't telephoned him when he beeped her, she had pulled a pillow over her head when they were in bed. She said, "I love you, I love you, and let me show you something I just got for you." She had bought Tarrant a card, and she took it out of her pocketbook. The words printed on the card were "I'm sorry for all the pain I've caused you." Tarrant read it while still holding the .22-calibre pistol in his hand.

"I won't go to jail," he said.

"I won't tell on you," she answered. "I'll go to the pay phone up the street and tell the police I got robbed."

Crystal walked out of the apartment toward the pay phone. Tarrant followed her in the van and parked it in front of another building. She called the police, and Tarrant drove away. When they arrived, she said she had been on her way home from a girlfriend's house and two men had jumped her in the street. The police drove her to North Shore Hospital, on Long Island. Her reflex action probably saved her life. The bullet had lodged in a bone of her hand.

A surgeon operated on her hand on Sunday. Crystal spent the night in the hospital and was discharged on Monday. Her left hand was in a cast, and she couldn't do much for herself. She was also afraid to return to her apartment. A year earlier, shortly before Crystal settled into her basement studio in Hollis, Florence Drummond had moved into the first apartment she had had since 1982, when she was evicted from the sixth-floor walkup on Sheridan Avenue. During the past year, Crystal and Florence had seen each other often and had become good friends. They went to clubs together. Florence went to Tarrant's store to keep Crystal company during the one or two evenings a week that Tarrant expected her to be there to keep him company. A drug-rehabilitation program that Florence completed in 1990 had given her a second chance at life—a second chance to be a mother to her children. On Monday, September 9, 1991, Crystal left the hospital and went to live in Florence's apartment. It felt good to her to be going home.

THE
BEAUTIFULEST
MOTHER
IN THE WORLD

When Florence Drummond gave birth to her first child, a daughter she named Crystal, on January 11, 1970, one month before her nineteenth birthday, she was living in an elegant gray stone mansion in Manhattan's East Seventies that had been converted into a home for unwed mothers. Crystal was born in New York Hospital. "It was lovely," Florence says. "And the next day you couldn't tell I just had a baby. I walked around that hospital hallway like someone who had never been pregnant. I was ready to go home." A few days later, Florence returned (with Crystal) to what had been her home until the sixth month of her pregnancy—the apartment of a friend in a housing project in Harlem.

Florence had met Crystal's father, Wesley Taylor, in the summer of 1968. She was walking from her friend's building to a store to buy cigarettes. When she passed him on the street, he said hello, "nicely." She ignored him. When she passed him on the return walk, he asked her name and whether she lived in the project. She answered. He kept coming around—he lived nearby, with his mother, Felicia Taylor; his father, Roderick Jenkins; and his younger brothers—and eventually they started dating. "Crystal's father was a real charmer," Florence says. "He swept you off your feet." She had been brought up in a strict manner, and Wesley was her first man. Wesley had spent most of his childhood in his mother's home town, Birmingham,

Alabama; had come North for his last year of high school; and had graduated in 1968—an A student, a part-time messenger, and a fairly heavy drinker. He worked as a full-time messenger until early 1969, when he enlisted in the Air Force to avoid being drafted into the Army during the Vietnam War. While he was still in basic training, Florence realized she was pregnant. She wrote to him about her pregnancy and hoped that he would marry her in August, when he was due home on leave before going to Korea, but he told her then that he didn't have enough money and that the Air Force might not approve of such a marriage. Florence knew that Wesley already had a daughter, Melanie, born in September, 1968, who lived with her mother in Delaware. What she didn't know was that Wesley was hoping to eventually marry Melanie's mother. Melanie's mother married someone else. "After that, his philosophy became to do unto others as they do unto him but let him do it first," his brother Nelson Taylor says. Wesley got another woman, Carol, pregnant while he was on a subsequent home leave; his son by her, Howard Taylor, was born in the fall of 1972. Florence claims she was "mad at first" about Howard's birth but got over it.

After Crystal's birth, Florence applied for welfare. Before her application was granted, she obtained the first of a series of jobs as a clerk-typist for lawyers and insurance agencies; she paid a Hispanic babysitter to care for Crystal during the week. She cashed the welfare checks she was sent without notifying the Department of Welfare that she was gainfully employed. When Staff Sergeant Wesley Taylor was discharged from the Air Force, in 1973, after a second tour in Korea and a few months in Vietnam, he and Florence and Crystal stayed at Felicia's for a while, then moved to a one-bedroom walkup on West 128th Street. There was a church nearby, where Crystal attended a Head Start program. There was also a small restaurant nearby, where Wesley took up with a woman named Barbara while continuing to see Carol—and others. Florence's next apartment with Wesley was on West 100th Street. Supposedly renovated, it was filled with rats "the size of cats," she says.

Wesley had become seriously addicted to drugs while he was serving overseas; his drug habit became even worse once he was back in New York City, and he never kicked it. He received unemployment insurance, and when that ran out he went on welfare. "Wesley led me into drugs," Florence says. "Heroin and cocaine." In January, 1976, she was laid off from her job; she supplemented her welfare checks by shoplifting. In August, 1976, Wesley and Florence's second child, a son they named Carlos, was born—gravely addicted to drugs. He developed pneumonia, spent a few months in the hospital, and went directly into foster care in the Bronx. Crystal remembers accompanying Florence to visit him. Carlos appeared frightened of Florence, whose skin is dark. He was less frightened of Crystal, who describes her complexion as "high yellow," perhaps (Crystal speculates) because the daughter of Carlos's foster mother had light skin. After Carlos's birth, Wesley, Florence, and Crystal moved to a two-bedroom sixth-floor walkup on Sheridan Avenue in the Bronx.

Florence was pregnant again a month after Carlos was born. In the spring of 1977, she was arrested for shoplifting, and it was discovered that there was a warrant out for her arrest on charges of welfare fraud in excess of five thousand dollars. In early June, she was sentenced to serve seven days on Riker's Island. As a pregnant woman, she probably wouldn't have had to do jail time for a first shoplifting arrest, but the welfare fraud was grand larceny. The week in jail covered both offenses. She returned to her apartment from Riker's Island, found women's underwear in her bed, tracked Wesley to a bar on 126th Street, and caught him kissing Barbara at the bar door. On June 30, 1977, Florence and Wesley's second son, Matthew, was born. "Call it a guardian angel, but Matthew was born free of drugs," Florence says.

As a veteran, Wesley Taylor was entitled to education benefits. While Florence was in jail, he enrolled in a community college, and spent some tuition and book money getting high with Barbara. After Matthew's birth, Florence stopped using drugs briefly and went to a business school, studying to become an executive secretary. She dropped out of school, because in order to get Carlos out of foster care she had to be home full time. Wesley's contribution to Carlos's release was to hold a job. He worked at a parking lot until Carlos came home, in 1978, and for a while afterward; it was the only job he ever had after leaving the service. Wesley had a second son with Carol as well—Roy, born in 1978.

Drug users and drug dealers frequented the apartments on West 128th Street and West 100th Street, but life took a turn for the worse at Sheridan Avenue. Of Florence's children, only Crystal can remember her as a sober working woman "before my father hooked her on drugs," and only Crystal has a few happy memories of Wesley. His terms of endearment for her were "baby girl" and "bugaloo." If her room was messy, he would say, "Damn, you is a dirty little heifer," but not without affection. When she was about five, he took her to her first circus, with Melanie—that was the only time she ever met her half-sister. He hit her just once, because she ran into the street and narrowly missed being struck by a car. Crystal also remembers that she had "all types of toys, dolls, and, after Mommy swindled a man she met in a bar out of some money he had stashed in his apartment, a new pink bicycle."

Crystal's childhood ended on Sheridan Avenue in 1977, after Matthew's birth. By then, Wesley was here today and gone tomorrow; he spent two or three nights out at a time, either at Felicia's apartment or at Barbara's, on West 129th Street. Florence resented Barbara for buying him away from her. Whereas

Florence received only a welfare check for herself and the children, Barbara also received a salary for working in a restaurant her family owned.

Florence often kept Crystal out of school to babysit—first for Matthew and then, after Carlos's release from foster care, for both boys. Crystal resented her mother's 9 A.M. to 11 P.M. absences. When Florence was home, Crystal was sometimes terrified that she might overdose. At the same time, she recalls, "I was usually glad she was high, because she enjoyed the high and left me alone. When she got her fix, she was the beautifulest mother in the world. We could do things that we couldn't do two hours ago. There was no doubt when she was high. She'd get into the middle of the street and start wiggling her butt and embarrass me. I'd rather see her like that than in the other mood. If she needed a fix, she'd get edgy and agitated, and when I said 'Mommy' she'd go *pow*, and hit me on the side of the head." Crystal eventually began drinking and using drugs—cocaine, PCP, mescaline—herself.

One evening when Crystal was about ten, Wesley and Florence had what Florence calls "a stupid argument that grew." Wesley started hitting Florence. He hit her until her eyes were swollen and her body was black and blue from head to toe. Florence remembers that he stopped hitting her only when Crystal jumped on his back and hollered his name. When she woke up, he was gone. He came back a few weeks later and apologized. "He said he didn't mean to do it and was sorry for how bad he had hurt me," Florence says. "I told him it was over." For the next ten years, Wesley lived with Barbara. Carlos and Matthew scarcely saw their father after that; when they did, they called him Wesley, not Daddy.

Florence had other men coming and going even while she was still taking Wesley Taylor's clothes out of or putting them into plastic bags on his comings and goings. In 1980, before Wesley left for the last time, Florence, approaching thirty, was seeing Clarence, a man in his late fifties. She had also taken up with a twenty-one-year-old named Leonard and, although she was using an intrauterine device, soon became pregnant with Leonard's child. She broke up with him, because she had good reason to believe he was sexually involved with Crystal. In the summer of 1982, Florence and her children were evicted from Sheridan Avenue for nonpayment of rent. Her furniture was taken by marshals. Florence promised Crystal she would get it back, but she was unable to make good on the promise. For a month, she and the children lived in a nearby basement apartment without electricity. From there Florence moved the children to Findlay Avenue to live with Hazel, a cousin of Florence's. Clarence had a room and a shared bathroom on nearby Grant Avenue. Florence moved in with him, returning most mornings to check on the children and most evenings to make sure they ate before they went to bed. Natasha, Leonard's daughter, was born in October, 1982. Florence's next child, James, whose father was Clarence, was born in February, 1984.

Clarence worked as a janitor in a nursing home on the

East Side. He was the best of the fathers of Florence's children: he drove them in an aged Cadillac to a bakery in Queens for day-old cake, treated them to fast food, and took them to the zoo. He bought Pampers for Natasha and, later, for James. He also bought drugs for Florence, although he used no drugs himself.

In the spring of 1985, not long after Crystal and little Daquan went into foster care, Florence checked herself into a hospital detoxification program. She told Clarence where she was—he promised her he would check on Carlos, Matthew, Natasha, and James every day after work—but she didn't tell Hazel. When Florence hadn't turned up for several days, Hazel called the police: she didn't want to be bothered looking after the children. The police came and took the Drummond children to the precinct and then to a hospital, where they were examined for signs of physical abuse. There were none, so the children were returned to Hazel's apartment. A couple of days later, Crystal's S.S.C. worker showed up there. He proposed giving Hazel temporary custody of Florence's children. Hazel's own daughter, who was twelve, had recently gone to school with bruises and had told her teacher that Hazel had beaten her up. When Crystal's S.S.C. worker returned to his office, he learned about the pending charges against Hazel. Until the child-abuse charges were disposed of, Hazel could not be given custody of anyone else's children.

Clarence let Florence know what had happened. She had been planning to have a hernia operation after completing the detoxification program, but the excitement caused her hernia to flare up. She was taken from the detox floor to the surgical floor to be operated on the following day. After a couple of shots of Demerol the pain subsided. The hernia was no longer a medical emergency, so Florence agreed to postpone the operation for two weeks. She telephoned the S.S.C. worker. He told her to come to his office. She showed him that she was still wearing a hospital band around her wrist, and explained what had happened. He said that because of Florence's situation—including her prospective return to the hospital—he would have to put her children into foster care. She signed them into placement voluntarily and asked the worker to keep the four children together.

In April, 1985, Carlos, eight, Matthew, seven, Natasha, two, and James, one, went to live with Mrs. Evelyn Peoples, in the Crown Heights section of Brooklyn. Mrs. Peoples, who was fifty, was separated from her husband. She was licensed for foster care directly by S.S.C. Mrs. Peoples had three children of her own—two daughters, who were in their twenties, and a fifteen-year-old son—living at home. When the four Drummond children arrived, she found them extremely undersocialized, lacking in self-control and manners, destructive with toys and her household belongings, and competitive with each other. In March, 1986, a month when her S.S.C. worker wrote that "all children have made an excellent adjustment to their foster care placement," Mrs. Peoples concluded that she could no longer keep Carlos; she wanted him removed from her home. For a year, he had been stealing money, comic books, and toys from the Peoples family, and had been disobedient at home and in school. There were two final straws for Mrs. Peoples: he had stolen two hundred dollars—the savings of one of her daughters—and Mrs. Peoples had learned from Matthew that Carlos had gone off at least twice with older men and received money in return for sexual favors. Carlos admitted that this was true.

Carlos was evaluated by a caseworker, a psychologist, and a psychiatrist. He was described in the evaluation reports as a tiny, bright-eyed, cute nine-year-old, who looked no more than seven. Carlos said that his mother had often taken him along when she bought and sold drugs and had had him perform sexual acts with her junkie friends in return for money or drugs. He foresaw an early death for himself from drugs from a needle. He thought his siblings might fare better, because they had not been with Florence so much. He had been beaten from an early age—with sticks and extension cords— and when Florence started to beat him she couldn't stop; Matthew had been beaten less. Carlos said that he had been left back in the second grade, and that neither he nor his mother had cared.

The psychiatrist thought that Carlos's basic average intelligence and his ability to talk about his life experiences were promising signs and made him an excellent candidate for therapy, but he didn't think Carlos could adjust acceptably to a normal foster-boarding home, and recommended placement in a residential treatment center.

In May, after Carlos was sent to a diagnostic center while awaiting placement in a residential treatment center, Matthew began stealing money from the Peoples family and destroying property. After testing, it was concluded that he, too, belonged in a residential treatment center. On July 1, 1986, both boys were admitted to Children's Village, in Dobbs Ferry, New York. Mrs. Peoples suddenly became ill, after the departure of Carlos and Matthew, and required hospitalization. S.S.C. was unable to find a foster home for two children on short notice, so Natasha was placed with a family in Queens and James with a family in the Bronx.

The detoxification attempt had failed, and Florence was too deeply involved with drugs—using them and selling them—to pay attention to her children in 1985 once they were in foster care. Not long after the children went into foster care, she moved her personal possessions from Hazel's apartment to Clarence's room. Crystal saw Florence regularly—she could travel alone to the old neighborhood and find her somewhere—but Florence did not show up for important events in Crystal's life, like her graduation from junior high school. Florence visited the four younger children at the Brooklyn S.S.C. office only twice in 1985. In December of 1985, Carlos, Matthew, Natasha, and James were adjudicated to be neglected; the neglect petition was for eighteen months. Florence scarcely visited her children during the first half of 1986, either. Crystal confided to her social worker at the group home that she was afraid her mother would lose her parental rights and that she was angered by her lack of interest in her children.

In July, Florence was informed that Carlos and Matthew were at Children's Village, and in August she went to see them. That summer, Crystal observed that Florence's stomach was growing. She asked her mother if she was pregnant. Florence, who was thirty-five, answered, "No, I ain't pregnant, I got a fucking tumor."

The phone rang at Crystal's group home on October 27, 1986. It was Florence. "You got a new brother," Florence said.

"You lying, you lying," Crystal said. "What happened to the tumor?" She later told a friend, "I was angry. It wasn't only that this lady told me a dumb lie but she already had five kids and a grandchild in foster care and for what she be needing a sixth child?"

To this day, Florence maintains that she had no idea she

was pregnant. "I was so high and the baby was so drugged that he never stirred," she explains. Two weeks before he was born, she had pains, but she was too strung out to think about them. On the morning of October 27th, Florence felt bad pains. She had an acquaintance call an ambulance. When it arrived, she got in and gave the attendant in the back her name. "Before he could ask me any more questions or take my blood pressure, I gave birth," Florence says. "I told the attendant 'Go get the baby.' When he asked me 'What baby?' I told him 'The baby between my legs.' He cut the umbilical cord, wrapped the baby in a white sheet, put him on my stomach, and wrapped another sheet around me and him. The attendant asked me did I have a name for him. I said 'No. What is your name?' 'Michael,' he said. 'O.K., that's his name—Michael.' Later, Clarence came to visit me in the hospital. He didn't ask me what I was going to do with Michael, because he had already asked me what I was going to do with James."

Michael was born with positive toxicity toward cocaine and spent six months in the hospital. He was then put directly into foster care with a fifty-eight-year-old woman in Brooklyn. While Michael was still in the hospital, Crystal often went there to feed him. The nurses assumed she was his mother, which led Crystal to believe that Florence didn't spend much time there. Florence didn't tell Carlos and Matthew about Michael's birth until February, 1987. She didn't know how they would react to the news.

Seventeen years earlier, in November, 1969, Florence learned that her mother, Lavinia Wilson, had just given birth to a daughter. She was even angrier than Crystal was in 1986. Florence found out about her sister Cynthia's birth at a baby shower being given for Florence when she was seven months pregnant with Crystal. Florence's mother and her two brothers had been invited. Her brothers came. She asked one of them where their mother was, and when he answered "Home with the baby" she asked, "What baby?" He said that their mother was delighted to have a daughter and was enjoying staying home with her, and he told her that Cynthia had arrived, at the beginning of the month, as a complete surprise. Lavinia had given birth abruptly, in her living room. At that time, Florence was eighteen. She had been in foster care since she was six years old.

Florence Drummond was born to Lavinia Wilson and Sylvester Drummond in New York City on February 12, 1951. Lavinia had had a son, whom she named Clifford, a year earlier, when she was nineteen. Lavinia, one of eight children born to Freeman Wilson and his wife, Rebecca, had grown up on a farm outside Memphis, Tennessee. She was raised poor. Her father was a farmer with a third-grade education; her mother worked in a laundry. Rebecca died when Lavinia was ten, and Freeman married a widow named Mabel. There were numerous step-relatives—children Rebecca had had before she married, children Mabel had had with her first husband. Lavinia attended segregated country schools through the ninth grade.

When Lavinia was about fourteen, the principal of her school arranged for her to go to Baltimore to "help a colored doctor and his wife" with their two small children and to attend school there. She was put back three grades. "They did that in the North to anyone coming from the South," she says. Lavinia considered the doctor's wife too strict and the schoolwork a waste of time, and returned home about a year later. In the summer of 1947, at the age of sixteen, Lavinia went to New York and stayed with step-relatives. "I got a house job taking care of a four-year-old boy," she says. "That lasted a number of years, until I got pregnant with Clifford."

Lavinia moved to a rooming house and went on welfare after Clifford's birth. She says that Sylvester Drummond "had a job as a housepainter when I first met him, but later decided he was too good to work." He abandoned her when she was pregnant with Clifford. He soon reappeared, she took him back, she got pregnant with Florence. They parted for good after Florence's birth, when she caught him cheating on her with "other womens," one of whom he later married. She believed that her life was deteriorating and sent the children to Memphis to live with Mabel, by then a widow. In 1953, Lavinia, still in New York, had another son, Samuel Wilson, by a man she had known in passing. No one in the family had been religious, but after Samuel's birth Lavinia came under the influence of a missionary, Winona Snowden, from a fundamentalist church in Harlem, whom she refers to as her "spiritual mother." She felt guilty about having had three children out of wedlock, started going to church most weekdays, several evenings, and for hours on Sunday, and describes the life she has led since as "a saved life."

Clifford and Florence returned to New York from Memphis in 1955; they went back there as children only once, for Mabel's funeral, in 1956. In the mid-fifties, Lavinia and her three children lived in a walkup on West 130th Street. They had a sparsely furnished bedroom and living room, and shared a bathroom and a small kitchen with the other family on the floor. There was a communal hot plate, but they had their own icebox—an old-fashioned one, which cooled food with a block of ice. The welfare check on which Lavinia and her children subsisted didn't go far. As Clifford remembers his youth, "Mom scraped pennies. There was no money for enjoyment, except a small black-and-white TV. No Christmas presents, no birthday presents, not enough clothes, and not too much to eat—sometimes just a can of spaghetti for dinner. Mom ate what we did." What Lavinia's children remember most about their early years is the churchgoing and the beatings. Lavinia often lost control and hit Florence and the boys with whatever implement was handy—an ironing cord, an extension cord, a doubled-up brown belt.

When the children played with the pan under the antique icebox into which the melting block of ice dripped, and spilled the water, Florence says she alone was whipped for the misdeed. Sometimes when just the three children were home, Florence ran away before her mother's return, to avoid an anticipated beating. She would either come home by herself or be brought back by the police. She appeared to be the target of her mother's guilt; Lavinia later told a caseworker that she felt compelled to punish her, according to "the Lord's direction." Lavinia also often forced Clifford to beat Florence.

A neighbor of Lavinia's had been threatening to tele-phone the New York Society for the Prevention of Cruelty to Children. Lavinia dismissed the threat, but it was carried out one day in late 1957, when the neighbor heard Florence wailing even louder than usual. Florence was removed from the apartment and taken to Manhattan's Children's Court, on East Twenty-second Street. Her body was a mass of bruises, welts, and cuts; one side of her face and one eye were badly swollen. Lavinia was ordered to appear in the court. Clifford and Samuel accompa-nied her. Two neighbors testified against Lavinia. She was found guilty of inflicting frequent and severe beatings on Florence, was placed on probation, and was referred to Bellevue Hospital for psychiatric evaluation and to the Harlem Hospital Mental Hy-giene Clinic for guidance. She and the boys went home; Florence did not. Florence was committed as a neglected child to the Bureau of Child Welfare. (By the time Florence's children went into foster care, B.C.W. had been renamed Special Services for Children.)

In December, 1957, Florence was placed by Windham

Children's Services, which specialized in temporary foster-home placements, with a young family in Brooklyn; she completed first grade while she was staying with them. Florence spoke to the caseworker about her dislike of the beatings she had received from her mother and about the lengthy church sessions she had had to attend with her; she said the emotional, frenzied worship frightened her. She also talked about the time away from her mother in the South. The caseworker believed that she was as healthy as she was because of the years she had spent with her grandmother.

In 1958, Florence's foster family went out of the state for a summer vacation, and Florence had to be moved. Windham chose another temporary foster-care family, who lived around the corner, so that Florence's life would have some continuity. She expressed pleasure in accompanying the foster family on excursions to parks and museums and in leading a fuller life with the new family than she ever had with her mother. During Florence's first year in foster care, Lavinia, Clifford, and Samuel periodically visited her in Brooklyn; the case worker noted that Florence appeared happier to see her brothers than her mother.

Florence's court-ordered indefinite stay in foster care was contingent upon Lavinia's psychiatric diagnosis and treatment. In March, 1958, the Bellevue psychiatrist who examined Lavinia had determined that she "could not be counted on to control her impulses" and that "the child, therefore, should not be with her." That year, Lavinia was also described by a case-worker as an "emotionally disturbed, immature person." When Lavinia was subsequently interviewed by caseworkers, she said "she felt that she was justified in whipping Florence and that she perhaps did not whip her with the right kind of article because the Judge had said that she should not have been thrashed with a strap." On another occasion, a caseworker reported, Lavinia said that a "neighbor complained that she heard only Florence being whipped, that wasn't true. She beat them all. So did the neighbor beat her own children. How else does one teach them right from wrong? The trouble was they had the strap in court. If they don't want her to use a strap, let them just tell her what to use." When Lavinia was asked what Florence did that pro-voked the beating, "she could not recall anything," the worker noted.

Lavinia Wilson kept some appointments at the Mental Hygiene Clinic, but when Florence was not returned to her she stopped attending the clinic. Because she showed no insight into her behavior, did not realize she had any emotional problems, and stated that she had no need for any type of casework or guidance, long-term foster care was recommended for Florence. In the second half of 1958, the Bureau of Child Welfare started looking for a permanent home for her. Despite Florence's "un-usually good adjustment to foster care," it took the Department of Welfare's Allocations Unit a few months to place her, be-cause there was "a lack of homes." In early December, Sheltering

Arms Children's Service, a Manhattan voluntary agency on East Twenty-ninth Street, placed Florence with Earlene and Benjamin Gardner.

On December 5, 1958, Florence went to live with the Gardners, in an airy, spacious apartment in a building with an elevator, off Convent Avenue in a middle-class section of Harlem, about fifteen blocks from Lavinia Wilson's two tenement rooms. Earlene Gardner's mother had been a foster mother since 1934. As she grew old and infirm, Earlene, a voice teacher who didn't marry until 1947, when she was in her forties, took over the foster children and reared them with the same philosophy: "Books and boys don't mix." A few Kodacolor prints, stamped "February, 1959" in red on the back, show Florence, wearing a frilly party dress, blowing out the candles on her birthday cake. The photographs have faded to sepia tones after thirty years in the Sheltering Arms files.

Almost the first thing that Florence's caseworker noticed about her was that she addressed Mr. Gardner as Daddy, while Marjorie, the other foster child in the household, called him Mr. Gardner. Perhaps because Florence was outgoing and appreciative, the worker concluded, she elicited a friendlier response from him than the "aloof" and "difficult" Marjorie did. To the worker, he was a "passive" figure. To Marjorie, he was a loathsome man. He worked irregularly, contributed little financially to the household, drank to excess, held it up to his wife that he was about ten years her junior, slept in a separate bedroom, refused to have his clothes washed with the children's clothes, and wouldn't eat with the children.

Lavinia, Clifford, and Samuel visited Florence in May and September of 1959, at the agency's office. Florence's reaction to seeing her mother was casual. She enjoyed seeing her brothers. Then the visits stopped for a year, for no apparent reason. Lavinia returned to the agency in September of 1960, without Clifford or Samuel. The Sheltering Arms caseworker asked where they were. Lavinia said she had sent them South, to a boarding school run by her church, because she had to work and couldn't take care of them after school. Lavinia wanted to know when she would get Florence back. Despite the adjudication of neglect, she claimed that the judge and the probation officer had told her that Florence's removal was only temporary. The caseworker asked her if it wouldn't be a better idea to have all three children with her in New York, rather than just Florence. Lavinia said no. Lavinia, then thirty, struck the worker as "a woman who appears to be in her late teens," and "appears to function well with her children out of the home, but to have much guilt related to the manner in which Florence was removed and is kept from her."

On December 29, 1960, Clifford and Samuel, who were home for Christmas vacation, showed up at Sheltering Arms with Winona Snowden, the missionary who had brought Lavinia into the fundamentalist Harlem church. Mrs. Snowden spoke at length to the caseworker. She said that she devoted much of her time to the "girls" she recruited and converted. In her opinion, Lavinia was so exceptionally orderly that she couldn't tolerate anything out of place, and when Florence would play and leave a mess, as children do, Lavinia would fly into an uncontrollable rage. Lavinia had improved since the boys went South. Mrs. Snowden had got Lavinia her present job, as a domestic for a wealthy family, for which she seemed suited. (She had done factory work, but factories often went out on strike.) The boys had grown during the three months they had been in school, thanks to better, consistent care and regular food. The Bureau of Child Welfare reviewed Florence's case annually, but kept her in foster care, because Lavinia never seriously sought her return home and never changed.

Florence has happy memories of attending Camp Mini-sink, in upstate New York, for several weeks every summer, and of participating in year-round activities that the camp held in Harlem. She liked watching television with Mrs. Gardner, going to the zoo, to church socials, and to the movies, and shopping. Food seemed to be her primary concern. (That was evidence of her "early deprivation," in one caseworker's opinion.) Her room contained many toys related to food—a refrigerator, a stove, dishes, cooking utensils—and she ate voraciously. After three and a half years at the Gardners', she was twenty-four pounds overweight. In her teens, she was five feet tall (that was to be her adult height), weighed a hundred and forty pounds, wore a woman's size-18 dress, and was mistaken for somebody's mother by one of her former caseworkers while she was visiting the agency. Dexedrine—an amphetamine with a high potential for abuse—was briefly prescribed for weight reduction by an agency doctor, but proved ineffective. Mrs. Gardner had difficulty finding youthful clothes to fit Florence, and sometimes resorted to friends' hand-me-downs.

Mrs. Gardner emerges from the hundred-page narrative of Florence's years in care (the pages reek of mildew after a quarter century of storage in Sheltering Arms' basement, and those on Thermofax paper are brittle and crumble at a touch) as a rigid person with troubles of her own. One of her most obvious concerns was money. In the nineteen-sixties, foster parents received a stipend of approximately a hundred dollars a month for each child and could submit a monthly expense account. Mrs. Gardner put in for twelve dollars and fifty cents after she had to call a plumber to extricate a piece of china from the toilet: Florence had broken a good plate without telling her. When Mrs. Gardner put in a request for five dollars to send Florence's trunk to camp ahead of her, the caseworker warned her that the agency would not pay for what it deemed an unwarranted expense. Within a year of Florence's arrival, Mrs. Gardner was pleading with the caseworkers for another foster child. Her pleas increased after Marjorie's departure, which had come about when Marjorie was caught shoplifting from two department stores, was sent to Bellevue for observation, and was placed, at her request, in a group home, because she had been beaten by Mr. Gardner.

Lavinia Wilson was originally informed that Florence was living on Long Island, and for three years she visited Florence at the agency. Mrs. Gardner, who was privy to this deception, said Lavinia could always be told later that Florence had moved: Mrs. Gardner had had a bad experience with home visits by one foster daughter's alcoholic mother, and preferred agency visits. In 1962, Lavinia Wilson was told the truth and was permitted to visit Florence at the Gardners' for an hour on the third Wednesday of every month. Although the visits went smoothly, Lavinia usually visited only every second month, and once didn't show up for five months; she explained that in addition to working full time she had been attending evening courses in typing and other subjects. Mrs. Gardner took it upon herself to invite Lavinia to special occasions, such as Florence's junior-high-school graduation and a Sunday-school graduation, and let Florence accompany Lavinia to a local photographer to have her picture taken in her graduation dress (an authorized ten-dollar expenditure). Lavinia Wilson said tearfully to a caseworker that she could not have done the job with Florence that Mrs. Gardner was doing. Mrs. Gardner told the worker that Miss Wilson stayed only an hour when she visited and "does not need to be told when to go." She described her as a very coöperative, considerate mother.

Florence expressed gratitude to the Gardners, but after three years with them she told her caseworker that she was anxious to return to her mother and had made a conscious effort to be good. Her mother had said that if she was a good girl she could come home. As the years went by, Lavinia continued to express a desire to have Florence return to live with her but always found an excuse, such as inadequate housing, not to have her do so.

Mrs. Gardner derived a great deal of satisfaction from her girls' academic achievement. Florence did well in grade school. Her intelligence was tested—it was average—and when she fell behind in some subjects in junior high school Mrs. Gardner sought tutoring help for her.

Florence left the Gardners' abruptly in June of 1967, at the end of tenth grade, and asked to be moved to another foster home. Up to then, her caseworkers had had only an inkling of the situation in the Gardner household. Florence is sure that they were as aware of Marjorie's beating as she was but let it go because Marjorie was perceived to be a wild child. (She later turned to drugs, and died at an early age.) Mr. Gardner had made sexual advances to Florence in a taxicab. He had wandered through her bedroom at night on several occasions. Mrs. Gardner had installed a lock on Florence's bedroom door, which she could chain from the inside. When the lock didn't prove strong enough, she advised Florence to put her dresser against the door, and, later, her trunk. In December of 1966, after Mr. Gardner started to call her at friends' houses and at Camp Minisink's library and, on one occasion, hit her, Florence ran away and went to stay with a friend named Virginia Miller, an older woman who had been raised by Earlene Gardner and her mother. Mrs. Gardner begged her to come back, and she did, temporarily, because, she says now, "of all the people in my life then, she was the one I took to best."

Mrs. Gardner had found it necessary to call the police on several occasions in order to insure her own safety as well as Florence's. As Florence got older, she learned that Mr. Gardner was accustomed to beating his wife. Once, when Florence was in her room, she heard her foster mother crying, "Stop, Benjamin! Stop, Benjamin! Benjamin, no!" As she recalls it, she went into Mrs. Gardner's bedroom, saw that Mr. Gardner had her down on the floor, went to the kitchen and got the cast-iron frying pan, and said, "If you ever put your hands on Mommy again, I'm going to kill you."

Florence spent a few days in June with Virginia Miller, and was then placed in the home of Shirley and Monroe Patten, an elderly couple in Yonkers, who also had a ten-year-old foster daughter, Dawn. For a time, Sheltering Arms considered the placement satisfactory—Mrs. Patten helped Florence acquire the habit of a daily bath and the use of deodorant, and supervised the selection of more appropriate clothes—but Florence was required to perform numerous household chores, while Dawn did nothing. She felt like an outsider, secondary to the spoiled, dependent Dawn, and stole money from Dawn's coin bank and from Mrs. Patten's bureau drawer. The agency arranged for visits at the office by Florence and Mrs. Gardner.

Mrs. Patten accepted this arrangement. What she didn't understand was Lavinia Wilson's lack of interest in her daughter: in
a year, Lavinia telephoned only once.

Florence completed the eleventh grade at Yonkers High
School, lost twenty pounds (Shirley Patten was a good cook but
put her on a diet), and missed city life. She had dated her first
boy, and he had introduced her to drugs, while she was with
Virginia the previous summer. As soon as school was over, in
June of 1968, she left the Pattens' house, without telling them
or Sheltering Arms of her plans. She went to Virginia's home
for a weekend, and then spent several weeks with another foster
sister while initial arrangements were being made for Virginia's
home to be certified as a temporary foster home for her. On July
29, 1968, the agency asked Lavinia Wilson, who was on vacation from her job, if she could provide a home for Florence for
a brief period, since foster homes were not plentiful for girls of
Florence's age, and she was regarded as too wholesome to be put
in a group home. Lavinia agreed to think about it for a few days.

On August 2nd, Lavinia telephoned Sheltering Arms.
She flatly refused to become involved, or to take Florence even
overnight, suggesting that the agency place her "where someone
can make her finish school and then she can go out and get
work." Lavinia spoke of the problems of teen-agers, late hours,
and going wild, and attributed the failure of Florence's placement with the Pattens (which she had heard about from Mrs.
Gardner) to Florence. Florence was devastated, and said to her
caseworker that she hated Lavinia—she referred to her as La-

vinia, not as Mother—and resented her obvious favoritism toward Clifford and Samuel. One reason Sheltering Arms certified Virginia as a foster mother for Florence was that in the agency's judgment Florence's real ties were to the Gardners' extended family.

Soon after Florence moved in with Virginia Miller, she met Wesley, and became pregnant during the spring of her senior year of high school. While she was pregnant, it seemed that she might need surgery for removal of a breast mass, and Lavinia Wilson's signature was required on a hospital operation consent form. When a caseworker spoke to Lavinia, in June, she asked, "Who's going to pay for it?" When she was told that the Bureau of Child Welfare would pay, she agreed to sign the form. According to the worker, "She seemed very much removed from Florence and what she was going through."

Florence's high-school attendance was poor during her senior year, and she had to take three courses in summer school; she graduated with a commercial diploma in August of 1969. The agency recommended that she move to a home for unwed mothers in October, 1969. Her case at Sheltering Arms was closed in March of the following year.

Though Florence envied her brothers because they were never in foster care, Clifford and Samuel hadn't had idyllic childhoods, either. The boys had to go to church with Lavinia every day. They were often beaten by the women who were "tarrying"—talking to God on their knees with their eyes closed, saying "Alleluia!" and "Praise be the Lord!" When the women rose to their feet, they would hit Clifford and Samuel. On their way to church, Lavinia, Clifford, and Samuel some- times passed Sylvester Drummond, a tall, thin man who looked to Clifford "more Hispanic than black." He used to hug Clif- ford and give both boys money for ice cream, but Lavinia always pulled them away from him, saying "He's no good." When Clifford asked if the man was his father, she said, "I don't want to talk about him," and "The case is closed."

Clifford had a problem controlling his bladder and often wet his pants on the way to church. He says that one night when he was about seven, Lavinia told him she had to punish him. She told him to go into the bathroom and drop his pants. While he held his genitals, she burned them with three kitchen matches, and then with three more matches, and then with three more. He still remembers the sight of the nine matches in the toilet. He remembers screaming. He remembers thinking that the real reason his mother injured him was that he reminded her of his father. Later, Clifford sought out a doctor at Harlem Hospital, and the doctor agreed to treat him without asking questions. Clifford didn't want his mother put in jail, nor did he want her to know that he required skin grafts and was having reconstructive surgery. He never told Samuel what Lavinia had done to him.

During their years at the boarding school, the boys

endured daily chapel and hours of church and revival meetings on Saturdays and Sundays—and a great deal of corporal punishment. Clifford was ten years old when they were sent there, and Samuel was seven. Samuel remembers that while he was stretched across a table someone on one side of the table beat him with switches and someone on the other side hit him with a razor strop. He was often tied to a chair with his back to a pole. Many nights, the mattress was taken off his bed, and he was tied to the springs. If Clifford cut him loose, both were beaten, and Samuel was tied to the bed again the next night. Both boys were periodically put in tubs of cold water with their hands and feet tied together behind their backs. Once, after being hog-tied and dumped in cold water, Samuel caught pneumonia. He was slipped into a nearby town, admitted to a doctor's office by the back door, and then taken to the hospital. For a while after that, he was treated nicely, but the whippings soon resumed. He and Clifford threatened to run away.

In 1964, when Clifford and Samuel returned from boarding school for the summer, they were able to persuade Lavinia not to send them back, because they really would run away. Toward the end of 1966, Samuel accidentally set fire to one of the rooms in Lavinia's tenement. All the family's belongings were lost. Lavinia and the boys moved to two rooms several blocks from their former lodgings, and later to an apartment on Jerome Avenue in the upper west Bronx. It was Lavinia's first real apartment—she had always lived as a roomer in other people's homes—and she was very proud of it. She obtained a bank loan through her employer in order to pay for furniture, was attending night school, and hoped some year to obtain a high-school diploma. A Sheltering Arms caseworker had observed that Lavinia's ability to read and write was limited.

After the boys' return from boarding school, Samuel went to junior high school and Clifford to high school. They ate grits and bacon and cereal for several years while Lavinia paid off their school bill, and resented the preachers at Lavinia's church, who ate steak. Clifford remembers that his mother celebrated making the final boarding-school payment by sending out for Chinese food.

In the fall of 1967, Lavinia didn't like the way Samuel was behaving. He fought with his teachers and his high-school classmates or played hooky; he was caught by the police riding in a car that had been stolen by one of his friends; he infuriated her by asking questions about his father. She took him to court, thinking that a threat of removal from home might make him respond to her discipline. It didn't, and in July of 1968 Samuel was committed by the court to Hawthorne Cedar Knolls School, a residential treatment center for emotionally disturbed adolescents in Westchester County. Samuel didn't have a bad time at Hawthorne; during his year there, he went to school, received therapy, learned to drive a backhoe, a bus, and a dump truck, and how to cook. In the summer of 1969, when he was sixteen and was ready to leave Hawthorne—he missed the city—he was given a choice of completing his high-school education or receiving vocational training. He chose to study industrial electricity. Though he has never been able to obtain his General Equivalency Diploma, he has been employed fairly steadily ever since he made that choice. Clifford dropped out of high school after completing the eleventh grade, and has also been unable to obtain his G.E.D.

Sometime during the ten years Lavinia worked as a housecleaner, she met a man named Rufus Parker, who drove the youngest child of her employers to school. Despite being "saved," and despite her church's disapproval of sexual relations outside marriage, she had sex with him. Clifford remembers seeing his feet in socks in Lavinia's bed before Cynthia's birth, and Samuel remembers seeing him there afterward.

Lavinia was "silenced" by her church for a year after Cynthia's birth: she was expelled from the choir, and had to sit at the back. She never rejoined the choir but resumed sitting in the second row. She didn't return to domestic work after Cynthia's birth. She stayed home, babysitting for the children of working mothers until Cynthia was old enough for school, and then went on welfare. In 1978, after their apartment in the Bronx was condemned, Lavinia and Cynthia moved to a housing project in Astoria, Queens. Samuel and Clifford had moved out in 1970, not long after Cynthia was born.

Lavinia has a photograph of herself with Cynthia, Crystal, and Wesley Taylor, taken on Crystal's fifth birthday. After 1976, Florence hardly saw her mother. Lavinia knew that she had become involved in drugs, and says she was frightened of her life style. Clifford and Samuel lost track of Florence after 1982, when she left Sheridan Avenue.

Children's Village, where Carlos and Matthew were sent in July of 1986, was founded in 1851, as the New York Juvenile Asylum, to shelter and educate vagrant immigrant children living on the streets of Manhattan. In 1901, the agency bought several hundred acres of land on a wooded hilltop in Dobbs Ferry, ten miles north of the city; the staff and children made the journey there by horse-drawn wagon. Today, more than three hundred boys, between the ages of five and sixteen, live at Children's Village, the nation's largest residential treatment center for emotionally handicapped boys. The boys are admitted primarily from four places: from more restricted settings, such as psychiatric hospitals; from homes where substance abuse, sexual abuse, and other forms of violence prevail; from homes with no abuse, but where some kind of assistance is needed; and from foster homes (some boys have been in as many as fifteen)—as Carlos and Matthew were, in July of 1986, when Carlos was close to his tenth birthday and Matthew was about to turn nine. Children's Village has been known to accept boys rejected by as many as fourteen other agencies. Currently, fifty percent of the residents are black, thirty percent Hispanic, twenty percent white and "other." They are housed in twenty-one "cottages," staffed around the clock. Upon arrival, each boy is evaluated by a multidisciplinary team, and an individualized treatment plan is designed for him. Most of the boys meet frequently with a social worker and a psychologist or psychiatrist. Most attend a year-round school on campus, which offers special-education classes, with a low teacher-to-student ratio. In addition to emotional and behavioral problems, the boys tend to have learning disabilities and to be several years behind grade level.

The staff at the group home where Crystal was living in 1986 did not pursue Florence. In January, Crystal reached the age of sixteen; in April, her discharge goal was changed, from discharge to biological mother to discharge to independent living. Fifty percent of the boys at Children's Village do return to a relative—Carlos and Matthew's goal. There is pressure on the agency to discharge residents within two years, and to involve parents in making a success of the treatment and in expediting the discharge, partly because the cost of maintaining a boy at Children's Village is about fifty thousand dollars a year. In February, 1987, Florence told Carlos and Matthew about Michael's birth—they took the news calmly—and signed a contract agreeing to attend a special weekly training course in parent skills at Children's Village. The contract read, "I will seek help and remain drug free, I will seek appropriate housing for myself and my children, I will apply for public assistance." (Florence had been taken off welfare when her children went into foster care.) "I understand that my failure to adhere to the above listed rules may result in termination of my parental rights."

Between March and June of 1987, Florence's attendance at the family-training sessions with Carlos and Matthew was inconsistent, and she occasionally appeared to be under the influence of alcohol: she always denied she had been drinking. Although she was briefly in another detoxification program that spring, she also denied any drug use. Nevertheless, she showed up with reasonable frequency and made a sufficient effort in the therapy sessions to be recognized at a graduation luncheon in June. At an early session, Florence confronted Carlos about his claims that she had taken him on drug deals and had him engage in sex with men for money. Carlos said he had lied. The child-care and social workers who were to work with him over the following years did not believe his denial.

That June, Florence, Carlos, and Crystal went to a state park on a picnic organized by Children's Village. In July, Florence continued to show up for family-therapy sessions, visited the boys on Sundays, and took them out for their birthdays. In August, she came two and a half hours late to one appointment and missed another. On August 19th, the boys' social worker asked her why she hadn't shown up on the twelfth. She said that when she was still dealing drugs, before her latest detoxification program, she had skipped with her supplier's drugs without paying, and had been dodging him ever since. He had finally caught up with her the previous week. He had beaten her and she had gone to the emergency room. She hadn't wanted the boys to see her so bruised. She was still slightly bruised on the nineteenth, under her eye and around her mouth. The social worker recorded what Florence said, and added that her demeanor and appearance had changed. The social worker was concerned that Florence was back into drugs. Florence wasn't seen at Children's Village during the month of September. In mid-October, she telephoned to say that things were going badly for her, and she still didn't come to Dobbs Ferry. In late October, her S.S.C. worker called Children's Village to say that Florence had also missed appointments with her and with Natasha, James, and Michael. Florence saw the younger children in November, but appeared helpless and hopeless about her situation—and high. That month, she told Carlos and Matthew that she couldn't give them a good Thanksgiving and would honor whatever decision they made about the holiday. The boys spent it with members of the staff at Children's Village. Florence had Thanksgiving dinner with Crystal at Crystal's group home. Crystal's psychologist noted (as he had often done before) that Crystal's mental status fluctuated with her mother's status. Crystal was having a difficult time because of her mother's condition and living arrangements—and so were Florence's other children.

The drug scene in which Florence had existed for a dozen years changed for her in September, 1987, after she started using crack. The drug affected her differently from heroin and cocaine: it made her high too quickly; it made her heart beat too fast. The world of crack was more violent and more sinister; she was frightened by the sight of crack dealers being held up and shot, and concluded that if she started selling crack she would wind up either in jail or dead. The increasing popularity of crack also deprived her of a living: users in her neighborhood were less interested in buying heroin and ordinary cocaine, which she had been selling for years. Because she had no money, she had to stay in Clarence's room all day. Clarence's landlord proposed raising his rent from two hundred dollars a month to four hundred dollars. He hadn't wanted Florence there in the first place: Florence was the first of Clarence's women Clarence had allowed to stay overnight. By then, Clarence himself had become fed up with supporting Florence's drug habit. He paid the landlord a little extra money, but he threatened to move out of the room on Grant Avenue and sleep at the nursing home where he worked.

Florence had recently heard of a residential drug-treatment program, Phoenix House, and told her S.S.C. worker she was ready to get away from drugs for good. The only way she could imagine kicking her habit was to move out of the old neighborhood. The first interview the worker could get at Phoenix House was in January of 1988. In early December, Florence was interviewed by Odyssey House. Two days later, she was accepted into its residential program. The worker had secured a bed for Florence at a shelter, because homeless adults are given priority in entering programs like Odyssey House, which tend to have waiting lists.

On December 10, 1987, when Florence went to Children's Village to tell Carlos and Matthew and their social worker about her imminent entry into Odyssey House's adult program, she talked non-stop and repeated herself endlessly. The boys appeared uncomfortable listening to her rambling speech, but said they were relieved that she would at least have a place to live and would not be "on the streets." Florence had deliberately got herself high, because she knew that that would be her last high from drugs. She didn't go to the shelter, but spent the night with Clarence. The next day, she moved into an Odyssey House building on Ward's Island. She was assigned to a room with six bunk beds. She went cold turkey. The first three days were the roughest: she was depressed and tired—she wanted only to sleep. After that, she felt better.

Florence was older than most people who enter the Odyssey House program for adolescents and adults: she was approaching thirty-seven in December, 1987. She had consequently been on drugs longer than most of those on Ward's Island with her. Once she had gone cold turkey, she never used cocaine or heroin again; all the urine tests randomly given to her afterward came back negative. Fifty-three percent of those who enter the program leave voluntarily (many because they are unable to keep away from drugs) or are dismissed for unacceptable behavior, such as "sexual acting out." Even passing notes, kissing, and winking result in a disciplinary talk. The dropout rate is highest during the first three months.

A critical part of Odyssey House's drug-rehabilitation program is to make residents confront the reasons for their addiction. Most of them have led lives of deprivation. A significant percentage have been physically abused, sexually abused, or severely neglected. Sixty-eight percent of the adults in the program are second- or third-generation substance abusers. Seventy-five percent of the female residents have children in the foster-care system or living with grandmothers. According to the president of Odyssey House, the men who fathered these children perceive their role as impregnating the women and carrying around photographs of the children in their pockets. Ten percent of the residents are white, sixteen percent Hispanic, the remainder black. Virtually all are poor. Odyssey House receives state and federal funds, but most residents qualify for public assistance, as Florence did. Their welfare checks pay for their room and board, and they are permitted to keep a small personal allowance from this payment.

Residents move through various levels toward graduation. Each level carries with it different restrictions, responsibilities, and privileges, which must be earned. When Florence was a Level I, she required a peer—someone else in the program at Level I—and an escort from Level III to accompany her when she went out. Only when she got to Level III could she go out alone. Level I's may write letters to their families; Level II's may make telephone calls to and receive visits from members of their immediate families. Level III's may get in touch with non-family members, visit their families with peers, and go on outings with them. Visiting one's children is regarded as a responsibility, so Florence was permitted from the outset to go with a peer and an escort to Children's Village to see her older boys and to the offices of the Child Welfare Administration's Division of Adoption and Foster Care Services to see her three younger children. (In 1988, S.S.C. became C.W.A.)

Florence is a guarded person. When she is questioned about her life, she finds it easiest to say "I don't remember," although she has an excellent selective memory. She tends to dismiss many questions with "I don't know" when she knows the answer but does not like it. In therapy groups, Florence was a good listener but a poor talker. Although her primary reason for entering Odyssey House was to get her children out of foster care as quickly as possible, it was many months before she was able to open up to others and deal with her feelings about herself, her family, and other people who had played a signifi- cant part in her past. Most Odyssey House residents who don't fall by the wayside during the first three months graduate from Odyssey House after a stay of between eighteen and twenty-four months. It took Florence two and a half years to graduate.

It became apparent early on that the main issue trou- bling Florence was the anger she still felt toward her mother for letting her be raised in foster care, and the anger and guilt she felt toward herself for having followed in her mother's foot- steps. She was required to submit weekly self-evaluation notes to her therapist at every level. In a note in May, 1988, in regard to Lavinia, she wrote, "I'm angry at the way she abuse me and now just like she did me I did to my children with the drugs." In mid-July, she wrote that she hoped "to see mother, sister, brothers soon and to let her know I still love her but was hurt by fact I had to be raised in foster home," and added, "I also want to let her know how it played a big part in me using drugs and how it is affecting my children now."

Florence reached Level I in February of 1988, and Level II in April. All program residents have jobs. Her Level I job was in the laundry. The staff believed she was isolating herself there; she was described until graduation as someone not given to socializing. Her Level II job was in the Admissions Department, which was in two four-story attached brownstones on East Sixth Street that housed the Odyssey House adolescent program. She remained on East Sixth Street, a site she preferred, until she completed the program.

Florence had not been permitted to bring her telephone-and-address book to Odyssey House. In the summer of 1988 she no longer had her mother's or her brothers' addresses or phone numbers, but she knew how to find her mother when she was ready to do so. On a Sunday in late August, together with a peer and an escort, Florence went up to the fundamentalist church in Harlem. She had no trouble finding her mother at the front of the church, where she always sat and sometimes stood, moving rhythmically to the music, punctuating the preachers' sermons with "Amen"s, and putting bills in the collection plates, which were usually passed five times during the Sunday service.

A week later, Lavinia, Clifford, Samuel, and Cynthia came to visit Florence on East Sixth Street. Florence's Level II therapist had told her just to discuss her uncles, aunts, nieces, and cousins, but Florence lost no time in confronting her mother about the past, and told her that on the next visit she wanted to see her alone. When Florence reproached Lavinia for letting her be raised in other people's houses, Lavinia told her that she hadn't chosen to put Florence in foster care and that she had sent Clifford and Samuel away because she couldn't bear raising them alone, without Florence. After four or five visits in the summer of 1988, Lavinia Wilson stopped visiting Odyssey House: Florence believes that Lavinia didn't care for her lines of inquiry. Florence reached Level III in November of 1988.

Lavinia's rejection continued to haunt her, and by April of 1989 Florence's commitment to therapy and her quest for the truth had deepened. One Sunday in April, she went up to Lavinia's church again. "My mother didn't greet me with open arms which I kind of knew she wouldn't," Florence wrote in a self-evaluation note. "And just by her actions toward me I now realize that she is not going to be the mother I want her to be. I felt like an outcast, someone she just had and that's it. I don't know why it meant so much to me to have my mother's love and to be accepted by her. Now . . . I know it's never going to happen."

Florence confronted Lavinia about her refusal to take

her in even for a night after she left the Pattens'. Lavinia said the agency had never asked her to do that. Florence was sure she was lying, because her caseworker at Sheltering Arms had told her what really happened on July 29th and August 2nd of 1968.

When Lavinia came to see Florence at Odyssey House in 1988, Florence had asked her to bring her some homemade chicken and some macaroni salad. Instead, Lavinia brought her Kentucky Fried Chicken she had bought. "I asked her why," Clifford says. "I asked her, 'Don't you love Florence? Isn't she your daughter?' She changed the subject real quick."

Lavinia maintains that the judge who removed Florence from her care wanted her raised in a home with a mother and a father. There is no evidence in Florence's record at Sheltering Arms that this is true, but Lavinia often says, "Look how much better the two I raised are than the one that was raised with a father and mother."

In 1988, Lavinia informed Florence and Clifford of Sylvester Drummond's death. Clifford concluded that she had known his father's whereabouts all along and had simply chosen not to reveal them. In 1989, Florence no longer remembered living in Memphis, but in 1961 she had told a caseworker at Sheltering Arms that she called her grandmother Grandma, that there were many people in her grandma's house, and that it was a very happy home. She said she had enjoyed eating a rice dish called mulattos, that she had entered kindergarten in the South, and that her father, Mr. Drummond—who was called Syl by others but Daddy by her—used to take her out while she was on the farm. In 1961, Lavinia Wilson also told the caseworker that when Florence lived on the farm she lived with her father, and that Sylvester Drummond was Lavinia's stepsister's husband. It was the worker's impression that Clifford and Florence were born while he was married to the stepsister. As a caseworker had noted on another occasion, Miss Wilson presents herself in the manner "of a child who holds a very big secret."

Samuel Wilson has never seen his father and knows nothing about him except his name. "You just don't want me to have a father," Samuel once said to Lavinia, in anger. His mother's answer was "I don't want anything less than going to church." Cynthia Wilson saw her father every now and then until she was nine, when she and Lavinia moved to Astoria. She hasn't seen him since. "I thank God that my children have stopped asking me about their fathers," Lavinia Wilson says. "I like being the mother *and* the father. All men are dogs."

In therapy at Odyssey House, Florence had to resolve another substantive issue in her life—the relationships with the three fathers of her children. She readily acknowledged that two of the relationships were not good. Wesley Taylor, the father of Crystal, Carlos, and Matthew, was her Pied Piper to drugs. "He didn't make me start using, but when I wanted to get off drugs he was the one pushing me further and further on drugs," she wrote. "Now he is strung out real bad." She had next to nothing to say about Leonard, Natasha's father. In the spring of 1982, when she was thirty-one, she had caught the twenty-one-year-old Leonard in Crystal's bedroom one day upon returning home unexpectedly. She was furious. At the same time that she believed Leonard was sexually involved with Crystal, who was then twelve, Florence was pregnant with Leonard's child; she felt betrayed by both Leonard and Crystal.

She felt differently about Clarence, the father of James and Michael. During the February after she came to Ward's Island, she said she missed getting her annual Valentine's Day card from him. That May, she reminisced that "this time last year he brought me a whole outfit for Mother's Day and I had dinner." Florence came to regret her treatment of Clarence, with whom she believed she had had a good relationship but one she had exploited. "I stole from him, lied to him, I did whatever it took just for drugs," she wrote. "The more he gave the more I wasn't satisfy." At first, Florence wondered if the feelings she and Clarence had formerly had for each other were still there. She subsequently said she learned in group that Clarence, whom she had considered "a father figure" (Clarence is twenty-eight years older than Florence), was nothing but "an enabler" for her drug habit. That wasn't the type of relationship she wanted with a man when she left the program.

Florence admitted in therapy at Odyssey House that she had been a "very sick mother"—the same words she used there to describe Lavinia. She resolved to make up for the years her children had spent in foster care as a consequence of her neglect, and for her failure to visit them after they were placed. "I knew the minimum I had to do to prevent the kids from being permanently taken away and being put out for adoption," she says. "And I did just the minimum."

From the time Florence started Pre-Treatment on Ward's Island, her first Odyssey House counsellor had agreed that she could continue to go to Children's Village for weekly family-therapy sessions with Carlos and Matthew. Crystal saw Florence every now and then, depending on her school or work schedule and the amount of time she was devoting to her boyfriends. Florence has never confronted her about Leonard, and though they have their ups and downs, Crystal and Florence remain fond of each other.

Florence was more concerned about the three younger children, especially the two boys—James, who had gone into foster care at the age of one, and Michael, who had gone into care directly from the hospital. "My last two sons I never even saw them grow up, or start walking or even cutting their first teeths," she wrote in a self-evaluation note in May, 1988.

Before foster parents are certified, they must agree to let birth parents see the children in their care regularly—usually once a week. The Child Welfare Administration's caseworkers for the children are supposed to arrange these visits. In the case of Florence's children, visits took place either in the Brooklyn office (Michael's foster mother, Geraldine Kent, lived in the Cobble Hill section of Brooklyn) or in the Queens office (Natasha's foster parents, Grace and Herbert Dunbar, lived in Springfield Gardens, Queens). Although James had been placed in the Bronx in 1986, his case was never transferred there from Brooklyn, so visits with him were also supposed to take place in Brooklyn but seldom did, because his foster mother found the long subway trip difficult. Toward the end of 1989, Florence prevailed upon C.W.A. to transfer James to a family in the Bronx that was amenable to bringing him on visits.

The children's C.W.A. workers changed rapidly. Whenever a worker left and a new one was assigned, weeks often passed before a visiting schedule was again established, despite the willingness of the foster parents to adhere to the visiting rules. Florence was troubled that Michael didn't recognize her and that neither of the younger boys was warm to her at first, although she acknowledged that she had no one to blame for the situation but herself.

When Carlos first came to Children's Village, in July, 1986, he had often been described as sneaky, moody, and depressed. By January of 1988, he had made significant progress. His social workers noted that he regressed only when Florence failed to keep appointments. He occasionally lied or was manipulative, but he was one of the most popular boys in his cottage. Matthew, although he was only ten months younger than Carlos, was babyish: he wet his bed, had frequent temper tantrums, and was afraid of the dark. Carlos, who tended to protect Matthew, was more accessible: he talked openly about his emotions, and he acknowledged Florence's drug addiction. Matthew was closemouthed about his problems and his mother's, and most reluctant to talk to adults. It was difficult for him to verbalize his feelings, but, unlike Carlos, who had been found to be learning-disabled and was behind grade level, Matthew was able to go to a public school in Dobbs Ferry and was never left back.

By early 1988, the behavior of both boys had improved so much since their arrival at Children's Village that the agency was prepared to discharge them. Carlos and Matthew realized that Florence's drug rehabilitation might take a long time or might not work out. They said they wanted to live with their sister Natasha's foster parents, Grace and Herbert Dunbar, who had offered them a home. It took many months for C.W.A. to approve the transfer—the agency tends to act slowly—but on February 28, 1989, Carlos and Matthew moved to the Dunbars'.

The Dunbars were then in their early sixties, and had been foster parents for twenty years. Mr. Dunbar, who worked for the Department of Corrections, is an old-fashioned man who prides himself on the fact that his wife has never had to work outside the house. They had raised Mrs. Dunbar's two sons, who are now in their forties, and a daughter. The Dunbars were eager to adopt one child who had been placed with them, but he was given to his grandmother—a placement that Mr. Dunbar did not approve of, because the woman lived in an untidy three-room apartment and "already had three other grands." Mr. Dunbar had been abandoned by his parents and placed in an orphanage at the age of five. "I was foster," he says. "I really missed a mother and a father, and I miss that to this day. Several people were good to me when I was coming up. I see foster care as a way of helping my people."

In 1969, four sisters, ranging in age from three to nine, came to the Dunbars from another foster home. In 1980, after the death of Mrs. Dunbar's daughter, the couple took in their eight-year-old granddaughter. She is now a college student. Three of the four sisters stayed for a number of years (the other didn't behave, and moved out), and Mrs. Dunbar is still in contact with them. "I get my cards on Mother's Day, they send, they bring, they come," she says.

When Natasha was transferred to the Dunbars' from Mrs. Peoples' home in Crown Heights, in 1986, Mrs. Dunbar unpacked her clothes in the back yard and shook them out, a procedure she followed with all new foster children. "I didn't have roaches and I didn't want roaches," she says. "Natasha had been in a typical foster home. Her clothes were ridiculous. The whites hadn't been washed with the whites, and the colors with the colors, so everything had run in together. She was a typical toddler. I couldn't keep a fan on the floor or flowers in a vase without her upsetting them, but toddlers are always touching and feeling—that's how they learn. It was up to me to see that her fingers didn't get tied up in a fan or her hands burned on the stove. That's a parent's job. Natasha wasn't well behaved when we got her, but she was a bright little girl and she wasn't no real trouble, and soon she was very good."

Natasha excelled in school. The Dunbars ordered Dr. Seuss books for her from a children's book club, bought her dictionaries, a bookcase, and a blackboard, and had the neighborhood candy store reserve a copy of a children's newspaper for her. From the bottom of the staircase they could hear Natasha in her bedroom teaching her dolls to read. Mrs. Dunbar was faithful about taking Natasha (and, later, Carlos and Matthew) to the C.W.A. office in Queens, and occasionally to the Brooklyn office to see Florence along with her other children. Once Florence had progressed enough at Odyssey House to be able to travel alone, they invited her to their home. "I never had no parents of foster kids come to the house except Florence, because I liked her," Mrs. Dunbar says. "When she said she would come, she would come. You set the table, she would sit and eat and not hurry. She stood next to our piano and sang. She had people who had cared for her." The Dunbars had no idea that Florence had been in foster care.

When Carlos and Matthew moved to the Dunbars', it was apparent that Natasha scarcely remembered them and wasn't happy to have them join her. "They came from a place with rough boys," Mrs. Dunbar says. The Dunbars gave Carlos and Matthew their downstairs bedroom ("The girls were upstairs with us, and boys and girls don't mix under our roof") and had no immediate problems with them. They were friendly, they did the yard work and other assigned chores, they were respectful. Although Matthew struck them as more intelligent, they preferred Carlos. "Carlos was neat," Mrs. Dunbar says. "Matthew had some nasty habits. He wouldn't take a bath unless you dropped him into the tub." Carlos was also honest, but Matthew lied and began to steal. "You couldn't lay nothing down because if you did, Matthew was gone with it," Mrs. Dunbar says. "He took my change purse out of my bowling bag and stuffed it into his eyeglass case. I found it when he put his eyeglass case down on the dresser and I could see it looked puffed up."

Early in November of 1989, the Dunbars were startled to learn that Carlos had been playing hooky. They were told that he had missed fifteen days of school in September and five days in October. They called Florence and suggested that she go to the school and talk to the principal. "Instead of me getting upset and fussing with my son I just politely went to the school Thursday morning to talk with the principal, the dean, and the guidance counselor," Florence wrote in a self-evaluation note. Like Mrs. Dunbar, who went to the school several times herself, Florence "couldn't understand how a child was able to stay out of school for fifteen days and no one saying anything. The only reason the foster mother was notified was because when my son played hooky in Oct. one of the teachers saw him."

At the end of November, the Dunbars had another shock. Carlos came home one evening with no clothes on under his coat. He told the Dunbars that he had gone to another boy's house with some friends, while the boy's mother was at work. The other boys had made him undress—he and his friends had taken their clothes off before at such gatherings. Carlos got angry and ran out of the house. He came home trembling with cold. Mr. Dunbar took him to the police precinct and filed a complaint. All the boys involved were summoned to Family Court, but nothing came of the inquiry. The Dunbars decided that Carlos would have to go back to Children's Village. He was readmitted there on January 30, 1990.

Matthew's sneakiness and stealing increased after Carlos left, and in the spring the Dunbars told their caseworker they could no longer keep him. Their C.W.A. worker stalled. In August, Mrs. Dunbar suffered a severe stroke. Mr. Dunbar couldn't take care of foster children and his wife, who would require several months in the hospital. He called his caseworker's office and explained his predicament, and was told to go home and pack Matthew's things. On September 12, 1990, Matthew Drummond returned to Children's Village. To the Dunbars' regret, Natasha had to leave them for another foster home in Queens.

That summer, Florence seemed to think it was time for her children to stop playing musical foster homes and for her to take the final steps to get them home. What she needed most was a job. Odyssey House Level III's are eligible for job training (if they need it) and are permitted to work outside the program. Florence felt good when she was sent to the New York State Office of Vocational Rehabilitation for evaluation in May, 1989. A month later, she was sent from O.V.R. to a business school run by the Federation Employment and Guidance Service, or FEGS, an organization sponsored by the United Jewish Appeal Federation of Jewish Philanthropies.

Florence had excelled at clerical work and, at FEGS, was pleased that tests showed she hadn't lost her aptitude for typing, filing, reading, or math. By the time she reached Level IV, in July of 1989, she was in school all day brushing up on a few rusty skills. In October, she officially completed school. Her job-placement counsellor at FEGS began to send her out on job interviews. There were numerous applicants for each secretarial position, and Florence wasn't hired. She acknowledged that many people had more experience—and more recent experience—than she did.

In late December, shortly after reaching the "reëntry" phase of the Odyssey House program, she was overjoyed to be offered a job as a secretary at an office-supply company, at a salary of sixteen thousand dollars a year. January 2, 1990, was her first day of work. "It was exactly fourteen years since I'd been laid off from my last job and lost all those years to drugs," she says. "It felt great to be drug-free and working."

In the summer of 1989, Florence had met a handsome twenty-four-year-old man named Burton who was at FEGS studying major-appliance repair. Florence and Burton were friends for six months and then became lovers. Level IV's have the privilege of dating anyone who isn't in the program. She spoke in group therapy of marrying him. Her therapist at the time thought that this was one of Florence's fantasies. Crystal hoped that the therapist was right. Once, when Burton was supposed to meet Florence and Crystal at a subway station, he showed up two and a half hours late. That December, Burton invited Florence to spend Christmas with his mother. At the last minute, he said there had been a death in the family, and the plans were cancelled.

Many Odyssey House residents who are ready to graduate are unable to find housing, since affordable housing is in woefully short supply in the city. Graduates have been permitted to stay on a month or two past their projected departure dates, because Odyssey House does not discharge its graduates to the street. It encourages some residents to seek housing in New Jersey and other outlying areas or to pool their resources and live with two or three other graduates. Florence is a city person; for her Ward's Island was "like being out in the woods," and she has an aversion to the suburbs. The only person she fancied living with, Burton, had told her of an available apartment in Staten Island near the one he shared with his mother. He had proposed moving in with her, so she gave Odyssey House a departure date—March, 1990. The apartment fell through. She took a single room with a shared bath and no kitchen at 104th Street and Central Park West, and left Odyssey House in early

May. She didn't go to her graduation ceremony on May 19th. Her diploma is still waiting to be picked up at Odyssey House's executive offices, on lower Broadway. Florence says she took the room in haste to get out of the program—she felt that it had nothing else to offer her. She was also five months pregnant with Burton's child. Florence wasn't showing much ("I was so big anyway"), but she didn't want her favorite therapist at Odyssey House to know she was pregnant.

She did tell Crystal about her condition. Crystal was even more exasperated with Florence for being pregnant in 1990 than she had been when she learned of Michael's birth, four years earlier. "Now this lady supposed to be finally straightened out, but she still got six children in foster care spreaded all over the map and she expecting a seventh," she commented disapprovingly to one of her social workers. "Where her head was at and what that young punk be thinking of?"

The original eighteen-month neglect petition, which was dated December, 1985, and stated that Florence had neglected Carlos, Matthew, Natasha, and James Drummond, had expired in June, 1987. It was then renewed twice, with Michael added to the petition. A C.W.A. worker asked Florence to sign her children into foster care voluntarily on June 2, 1989. Florence wasn't yet in a position to take her children out of foster care, but she was working toward that goal: she was doing well in her Odyssey House program and was visiting the children regularly. The purpose of having Florence accede voluntarily was to ease the way for her to get her children back.

The judges who serve on the Foster Care Review section of New York State's Family Court in New York City review cases for the city's five boroughs. On October 4, 1989, a 358A hearing—the initial review of a voluntary-placement agreement—was held in Family Court. A 358A hearing has several objectives, among them to certify that the voluntary-placement agreement was not signed under coercion, and to set a date for the next review of the case: the date set on October 4th was December 4th. At the 358A hearing, an organization called CASA—Court Appointed Special Advocates—was assigned to monitor the case of Florence and her five younger children; CASA accepts only cases in which children were placed voluntarily in care. A Foster Care Review judge may hear sixty or more cases each day. CASA's staff and volunteers assist an overwhelmed court to facilitate the exit of children from foster care by supplying judges with relevant information, and assist parents and children adrift in the child-welfare bureaucracy in the same way, with information that their overwhelmed caseworkers often do not have.

Deborah, the CASA volunteer assigned to Florence in October, 1989, got in touch with her at Odyssey House just as she started to search for a job. Two months later, when Florence had begun working, Deborah cited housing as the main obstacle preventing Florence from regaining custody of her children. In

1987, the caseworker who helped Florence apply to Odyssey House had also helped her apply to the New York City Housing Authority for public housing and for a Section 8 housing subsidy. (Section 8 is a federal program that provides low-income people with vouchers to pay part of the cost of private housing they could not otherwise afford.)

By early 1990, neither apartment nor vouchers had materialized, and Florence's caseworker was no longer with C.W.A. The agency had, however, created a new housing-subsidy program, to reunite parents with children in foster care when the foster-care worker determined that a lack of adequate housing was the primary factor preventing discharge. The maximum amount of assistance an eligible family could receive was three hundred dollars a month for as long as three years. Deborah called Florence's latest C.W.A. caseworker to have her apply for the subsidy for Florence, but the caseworker knew nothing about it and asked Deborah to send her the information.

In June, 1990, Deborah learned that Florence had been living since May in the room on Central Park West, for which she was paying six hundred and eighty dollars a month. She also learned, later that month, because Florence had initially confided in her C.W.A. caseworker, that Florence had been pregnant and had just lost the baby, at six and a half months. In July, Florence admitted to Deborah that she was in bad financial shape. She had been out for three weeks as a consequence of the miscarriage and had lost two weeks' pay, because new employees received only one week of sick leave.

Deborah went on vacation in August, 1990. She returned in September to discover that Florence had yet another C.W.A. caseworker and that nothing had been done to assist her in finding housing. When CASA (the New York City branch is one of four hundred CASA programs nationwide) is assigned a case and believes that the client needs counsel, it seeks legal help. Deborah had already called a lawyer in the civil division of Legal Aid to ask if Florence met the criteria for him to assist her. Another tenant in the building on Central Park West had told Florence that, at six hundred and eighty dollars a month, she was being overcharged for her room. The other tenant was paying less than a hundred and fifty dollars a month for a similar room. Legal Aid was limited in what it could do for Florence. Every child in foster care in New York State has a law guardian, and Legal Aid's juvenile division represents ninety-nine percent of these children, including Florence's. To represent their mother would be a conflict of interest. Legal Aid suggested that Florence confront her landlord about her rent, and referred her to Morningside Heights Legal Services, a small clinical program run by Columbia University Law School. In September of 1990, two second-year Columbia law students and a social-work student were assigned to Florence to help her obtain financial assistance for an apartment.

On October 9th, fortified by this legal support, Florence confronted her landlord over her excessive rent and explained her need for a decent-sized apartment for herself and the children. She told him she had gone to a lawyer. The landlord said that he couldn't read her mind about requiring larger quarters and gave her twenty dollars for carfare to look at a newly rehabilitated four-room apartment in a building he owned in the Sunset Park section of Brooklyn. It rented for seven hundred dollars a month.

Florence took a one-year lease for the apartment to Morningside Heights Legal Services. The students knew that Florence was also eligible for a "one shot" public-assistance grant. They told her what documentation she would need, got her an emergency appointment at a public-assistance Income Maintenance Center, and spent a whole day sitting there with her. Without the grant, Florence, with no savings, could not have afforded the apartment. Within twenty-four hours, Florence received a check for a month's security deposit and her first month's rent.

C.W.A., having been educated by Deborah about its own three-hundred-dollar-per-month, up-to-three-years housing-subsidy program, put through a grant for Florence. Morningside Heights found an agency near her new apartment, the Center for Family Life, to supply continuing support services. Florence and her children would eventually go there for therapy.

Morningside Heights Legal Services also encouraged Florence to apply for Medicaid and food stamps (for which, because she had several children, she would be eligible despite her salary), and other subsidies, of which she had been unaware, including an allowance for furnishings and supplies required to establish a new household, which provided her with a few hundred dollars. Each child released from foster care was also entitled to a five-hundred-dollar discharge grant from C.W.A. for furniture and other items deemed necessary to make the child comfortable.

The Columbia students take on only two or three cases a year, so that they can devote sufficient time to each. Because Florence said she was determined to continue working full time, they helped her obtain services she would need once her children came home, including after-school care for James (a first grader) and Natasha (a third grader) and day care for four-year-old Michael. The five hundred dollars for each of Florence's children was disbursed by C.W.A. in a timely fashion. The agency had learned that with CASA advocating for a client, it would be taken to court for failure to fulfill its obligations. Florence moved into her new four-room apartment on October 20, 1990. All the subsidies paid out to her by C.W.A. and the other agencies involved were far less than the cost to the city of keeping her children in foster care—a minimum of twenty thousand dollars per child per year.

Carlos had settled down quickly after his return to Children's Village from the Dunbars'. His social worker, his mother, and Deborah all expected him to be the first of the children to be "trial-discharged": children coming out of foster care are returned home provisionally, and if after three months they seem to have adjusted well they are given a final discharge. The social worker believed that Carlos was ready to return home in the fall of 1990, but, to her surprise, he told her he did not want to go. He chose instead to enter a group home that Children's Village had recently opened near Dobbs Ferry. His social worker believed that it would be destructive to attempt to discharge him to Florence against his will. Florence, who was taken completely off guard, was stunned and hurt, but had to accept his decision.

Natasha was anxious to be with her mother. It was decided that she would be the first discharged: one child had to be discharged within sixty days of the mother's receiving the C.W.A. rent subsidy; James and Michael would follow. Carlos and Matthew came down from Children's Village most weekends and holidays. When Florence yelled "Hammer time!" or "Work time!" they nailed down linoleum or put up curtains. Florence was chosen to receive a Children's Village Thanksgiving food basket, and cooked a hearty turkey dinner that included stuffing, greens, and sweet-potato pie. All the children were there for Christmas Day. Florence had saved up to buy nice presents. She bought a small plastic tree and decorated it with ornaments and tinsel.

On December 5, 1990, sixteen days before Florence's younger daughter, Natasha Drummond, eight, went to live with her, Florence's older daughter, Crystal Taylor, twenty, was discharged from foster care by St. Christopher-Ottilie, and moved into a basement apartment in Queens. Crystal was peeved with Florence, who told her she was pregnant yet again, and with Burton, who was seldom around, "except to whisper sweet nothings in Mommy's ear." Florence later learned that she was not pregnant after all, but had an enlarged uterus.

Crystal's father called her on January 11, 1991, her twenty-first birthday. A few months earlier, Wesley Taylor had left the apartment in Harlem that he had shared with Barbara for ten years, because Barbara's income had plunged. The restaurant where she worked had been closed for selling drugs. She could no longer afford to keep Wesley high enough. He had moved into his mother's one-bedroom apartment in a project in the Williamsburg section of Brooklyn. Two of his brothers also lived there, with Felicia Taylor: her son Nelson, who was in a drug-rehabilitation program, and her son Lloyd, who was not. Lloyd or one of Wesley's other brothers supplied Wesley with drugs. He told Crystal to come by the apartment and he would give her some birthday money.

On Sunday, January 29th, Crystal rented a car and drove Carlos and Matthew (who were visiting from Children's Village), Natasha, and James (who had just been trial-discharged from foster care) to her grandmother's apartment. Wesley Taylor looked awful. "Old and drugged out" was the way Crystal saw him. She asked him for her birthday money and was disgusted when he told her he had spent it, and how: "I needed a hit." Crystal had always loved her grandmother but had had only contempt for Felicia's sons. "Ain't none of them was no role models for me to look up to," she said that night. "They was no doctors, lawyers, no sheriffs, no people to keep me out of foster care."

Crystal had been upset in January by little Daquan's having lied to his teacher about Mrs. Hargrove, which had led to his return to the Bronx to live with big Daquan.

Florence had also received upsetting news in January. Because of the recession, her employer had reduced her hours from thirty-five to twenty a week. That meant she would have to reapply for welfare to make ends meet.

As Florence's children were being discharged from foster care, she made it clear that her idea of motherhood was similar to Crystal's: let the former foster parents keep the children as often as possible. For Easter Week in 1991, she sent Natasha to the Dunbars', and James to the home of Jacqueline and Lamont Charles. The Charleses had become James Drummond's foster parents in November, 1989, when Florence had him removed from the home of the woman who would not bring him to Brooklyn for visits.

The Charleses, a retired couple in their sixties, whose two children were grown, lived in a well-kept town house on a quiet street. Mrs. Charles became a foster parent in 1988. The Charleses had a thirteen-year-old grandson, Norman, who had been with them much of his life, and they decided that they would keep two boys as company for him. When James arrived, the Charleses had Melvin there and after Melvin left to return to his family they took in Timothy; James and Timothy especially liked playing in the Charleses' finished basement, which they called their apartment. Mrs. Charles enjoyed being a foster mother. "It's not something you do for money," she says. "Who would want to take care of a child seven days a week for a hundred dollars, which is what it comes to when C.W.A. gives you four or five hundred dollars a month?"

The foster boys called Mrs. Charles Grandma and Mr. Charles Grandpa, because their grandson did. "Sometimes you get so attached to them you do more for them than for your own," she says. "You're supposed to. I was working when my son and daughter grew up, so my mother-in-law took care of them. Therefore, I'm going to take good care of these children."

After James returned to Florence, the Charleses sent him "a little piece of money" for Valentine's Day and another little piece for his birthday. When Florence called to ask if James could stay with them for Easter Week, they agreed. Carlos took him partway to the Bronx by subway; the Charleses met him and took him the rest of the way. They were disappointed that Florence had sent him without an Easter basket and without a haircut. They bought him an Easter basket—"to make his Easter"—and had his hair cut: it had been cut every two or three weeks while he was with them.

Mrs. Charles found in James's notebook a list of things that he was supposed to ask the Charleses for. The list that Florence had given him read "I want a haircut, I need sneakers, I need a book bag, underwear, and clothes." When Mrs. Charles discovered the list, she had already bought James a book bag and "a two-piece underwear, because I wanted him to have that." She didn't buy him sneakers or any other clothes. The Charleses had subscribed to *Highlights* magazine for James, and at Easter they gave him the copies that had come since his January departure. Timothy cried when James left after Easter, so Mrs. Charles took in another foster child, Marlon. When Florence telephoned in June to ask if James could visit for a few weeks in the summer, Mrs. Charles told her that Timothy and Marlon had left and she had given up foster care. "You should have heard Florence in 1989 at the meetings with the people from C.W.A. and the court-appointed ones saying how bad she wanted the children," Mrs. Charles says. "I'm sure she's a good mother, but she still wants to have a good time. If she can get the children off her hands, that's fine, but I didn't like the way she went about it."

Michael came home after Easter. Sitting at the dinette table one Sunday afternoon eating peanut-butter-and-jelly sandwiches with his sister and brothers, he repeated to himself, "Mommy Florence Drummond, Mommy Florence Drummond." He appeared happy playing and watching TV with James and Natasha but told one of his older siblings that he didn't like Mommy and wanted to be with Ganny, which was what he had called Geraldine Kent for the four years he was with her.

At the suggestion of her sister-in-law, Mrs. Kent had become a foster mother in 1968, after Jeffrey, the second of her two children, had some serious asthma attacks when he was eight, which required her to take a leave of absence from her job in a pickle factory. (She had separated from her husband soon after Jeffrey's birth.) Mrs. Kent has had numerous foster children since. She adopted Thomas, the second child placed with her; he is now twenty-two years old and still lives with her. In 1982, she took in a baby boy, Otis, who is mildly retarded. When Otis was four and became eligible for adoption (his mother had disappeared), Mrs. Kent adopted him. Michael and Otis had been playmates since Michael came to Mrs. Kent's apartment—a two-bedroom one in a project—in early 1987, as a baby. Mrs. Kent's divorced daughter and her two children, who are twelve and eighteen, visit often. When Michael is with Florence, he recites the names of the children and young adults who make up his world at Mrs. Kent's.

"It was hard for me to let Michael go," Mrs. Kent said recently. "When he went home, I told him, 'Mike, you be a good boy,' and turned away, so he wouldn't see me crying.' I told Florence, 'You better not let anything happen to my baby.' "

As it turned out, Mrs. Kent did not have to let Michael go. He is the only one of Florence's children who has two homes. For the past year and a half, Geraldine Kent has kept him two or three weeks in summer and for a week or two over other school holidays. Mrs. Kent's welfare check covers her rent, which is low; her phone bill; and the gas and repairs for her 1980 car. Florence has never been to Mrs. Kent's apartment and has never offered to keep Otis, but Mrs. Kent doesn't mind. She is grateful to have Michael whenever he is able to come. He strikes her as a little more spoiled and a little readier to cry than when she had him, but if she asks him to do something and he refuses she threatens to send him home, and he says, "I'll be good." When it is time to leave Ganny, he asks "Why do I have to go home?" but, once home, he is soon playing with his older siblings.

In mid-August, 1991, a couple of weeks before Tarrant had shot Crystal, she happened to run into her uncle Nelson Taylor on the subway. He told her that her father was in the Veterans' Administration Hospital in Manhattan. Crystal, Carlos, and Nelson went to visit Wesley Taylor in late August. Wesley told Crystal that he had AIDS. It was his illness rather than his drug use that had made him appear so wan when Crystal saw him in January. Wesley Taylor died on Thursday, September 12th. It had been his custom to telephone Crystal every once in a while to "talk trap." One evening that summer, he had called her, had assumed or pretended to assume that she was with a man, and had said, "Tell that nigger to roll off you, this is your daddy." His parting words to her when she said goodbye to him at the V.A. Hospital were "Go on, little ho, and bust one for me."

Wesley Taylor's wake was held in a storefront funeral home in Harlem on the evening of Sunday, September 16, 1991. The open coffin was at the front of a plain room filled with chairs. Florence and the children filed past. Crystal was fashionably dressed in a black silk tank top, white culottes, a black plaid jacket, and a black-and-white hat, but she looked worn out from the combined trauma of the shooting and her father's death. Inside the cast, her hand throbbed with pain. Crystal burst out sobbing. "Daddy, Daddy, I never thought I'd see you like this," she wailed at the gaunt figure in the casket, a shadow of the nice-looking Don Juan she remembered from her childhood. "How could you leave me this way?" Matthew Drummond was quiet. Carlos confided to a male friend of the family who attended the wake that he felt sad he had never had a father. "Wesley kept saying he was going to come around and see us, and he never did," Carlos said, in an uncustomarily plaintive tone. There was a single basket of white flowers in the room, between the coffin and the visitors' book. It had a card that read "From your sons Howard and Roy."

About fifty people attended the funeral, which was held the next morning in the same room. A second floral tribute, this one of red flowers, stood next to the first. Some neighbors of Wesley and Barbara's from 129th Street had taken up a collection to buy it. The person who sobbed the loudest was Barbara. She sat in the back, a homely woman who was much heavier than Florence.

The most surprising person in attendance at the funeral

home on that heat-heavy mid-September day was Lavinia Wilson. Lavinia had learned of Wesley's death that morning. She
later told Florence she had made the journey from Astoria
because she had known him. A soft-voiced minister the family
had never seen before spoke briefly. "Life is not a round trip,"
he said. "It's a one-way street to death. Wesley Taylor has now
gone from life to life everlasting."

On the day of the funeral, Lavinia Wilson, still slender
and wearing a pretty church dress and one of her many pretty
church hats, asked her grandchildren what they wanted for
Christmas. Lavinia did buy the children Christmas presents, and
was surprised when Florence and Crystal gave her a hat and
Cynthia gave her a suit. As Florence had predicted, she would
never be accepted by her mother. Florence continues to envy
Cynthia, the favored daughter, who until recently lived with her
three-year-old son in her mother's apartment. Cynthia and her
son now have an apartment of their own in the Bronx. Like
her mother, Cynthia, who was nineteen when her child was
born, was silenced by her church for one year for having a baby
out of wedlock. Before she moved out, she attended church
every Sunday. Florence's brother Clifford turned to crack in the
mid-eighties. He had no place to live, and moved in with Lavinia
and Cynthia in 1987. He stayed there for three years. While he
was with them, Lavinia beat Cynthia severely, and on more than
one occasion Cynthia went to stay with Samuel Wilson and his
family for a couple of months. When Florence first got out of
Odyssey House, she asked Lavinia if she could visit her in

Astoria; she has stopped asking. Lavinia initiates few phone calls and usually confines her travels to her part-time job at a discount store and to her church.

For six weeks after her father's death, Crystal lazed around Florence's apartment watching sitcoms, cartoons, and soaps and "conversating" on the phone. She appreciated the opportunity to be with Natasha, James, and Michael: "Now they knows that I am they big sister, Crystal." Since 1989, she had worked in the mailroom of an advertising agency on Madison Avenue. The agency was paying her disability insurance for three months. Tarrant drove Crystal to her doctor's appointments; her hand healed well, but the bullet left a bad scar. Tarrant told her he would take care of her rent and some other bills—the recession had cut into his income, he said—until she got back on her feet.

When Crystal went to her apartment to get her mail on October 25th, she discovered that it had been burglarized: her TV, her VCR, and a telephone that Tarrant had given her were missing. In early November, Tarrant drove Crystal's furniture and other possessions and her spring and summer clothes to a five-by-ten-foot storage room and paid six months of eighty-dollar-a-month storage charges. He had paid Crystal's September and October rent. Her month's security deposit covered the November rent.

The day after visiting the apartment, Crystal learned from an acquaintance that she could earn fifteen hundred dollars if she would marry an illegal alien, convince the Immigration and Naturalization Service that it was a bona-fide marriage, and stay married to him until his visa was stamped in a way that permitted him to leave the country and return. Crystal needed the money to pay off clothes bills and rental-car charges she had put on her credit card. She was to marry a Moroccan in his late thirties, and Florence, who was also in financial straits, would marry a Nigerian in his early twenties. Crystal met the Nigerian and liked his looks. "You be getting this fly husband and I be getting another senior citizen," she observed to Florence. Ultimately, it was Crystal who married the Nigerian—and had a brief romance with him—and Florence the Moroccan. Crystal was paid in full for her marriage. Florence received only five hundred dollars' advance money; the marriage broker absconded with the remaining thousand dollars.

Florence's financial problems had begun after she applied for welfare. At first, she received $313.20 a month and food stamps worth $271. Then the computer at the public-assistance office turned up the fact that Florence still owed money on her earlier welfare fraud: serving the week in jail in 1977 hadn't wiped out the debt. The office was also under the mistaken impression that all Florence's children were still in foster care. As the months went by, her welfare checks got smaller. By summer, she was receiving $72.60 a month and food stamps worth $401. The food stamps didn't pay the rent, and she couldn't pay it with her part-time salary and the small welfare checks, either. (She did take advantage of supermarket specials, and stockpiled groceries.) By the end of the year, Florence owed her landlord twelve hundred dollars—her share of three months' rent. The landlord obliged her by filing a dispossess—a document that states the amount of rent the tenant owes and threatens the tenant with paying up, appearing in court, or moving out. Florence and her landlord knew that when she went to court the rent would be paid, because the city has a mandate to prevent eviction if children are endangered.

Pamela, Florence's social worker at the Center for Family Life in Sunset Park, which a number of child-welfare professionals consider one of the best preventive-services agencies in the city, was trying to help Florence straighten out her finances. Florence, Natasha, James, and Michael met with Pamela at the center every Monday evening, and Florence was persuaded to join a single-parent group session on Thursday evenings. One evening when Florence arrived at the center, Pamela told her that she had been flabbergasted to learn from the director of the local public-assistance office that Florence was married. The director had told Pamela that her client had a nerve asking public assistance to pay her rent when she was swindling the taxpayers by getting rich from a foreigner. Pamela asked Florence why she hadn't told her about the marriage. For once, Florence came right out and admitted what she had done, and why. She told Pamela that she had received only five hundred dollars, and had spent a lot of that to buy the children clothes. The director agreed to pay the back rent and to close Florence's welfare-fraud case. Florence's latest experience with welfare convinced her that she would be better off working full time, and when full-time jobs again became available at her company, in February, 1992, she accepted one. By then, Florence didn't have to worry about rushing home to pick up her children from after-school care at six o'clock. Matthew Drummond, fifteen, had been released from Children's Village just before Christmas, 1991. He had been caught stealing from other boys in Dobbs Ferry after his return there from the Dunbars', in September, 1990, and from Florence when he came home on weekend visits early in the year, but then the stealing had stopped. He was happy to come home and also attended the Monday-evening therapy sessions—a requirement during his three-month trial-discharge period—although he was even more guarded than his mother.

Florence has been depressed in recent weeks. In order to be eligible for food stamps and other benefits—and because she still hopes to marry Burton—she paid five hundred and seventy-five dollars to get a divorce from the Moroccan. Sixteen-year-old Carlos had appeared to be doing well at the Children's Village group home near Dobbs Ferry until December of 1991, when he started to bully the younger boys and to provoke fights, threatened to damage a staff member's sports car, and punched holes in walls. In the opinion of his social worker, part of his behavior was attributable to his father's death. He was sent back to Children's Village for a while, and, then, in the summer of 1992, was transferred to a Children's Village group home in Flushing. He is smoking reefer, sleeping with girls (he says he uses condoms, because "I don't want to be no one's father"), and cutting some classes. He goes to Florence's apartment fairly often on weekends, but his discharge goal is "independent living." He recently visited the Dunbars. "I won't go home unless I foul up and have nowhere else to go," he said to Mrs. Dunbar. "There's something about my mother that isn't quite right."

As Carlos seemed to adjust to Flushing, Matthew began to behave in ways that were unacceptable to Florence. When he was supposed to pick up the younger children after school, he showed up late or not at all. He was defiant. Florence found the windows of her apartment open and large amounts of bread, juice, and eggs missing from her refrigerator. The younger children found a bottle of beer under his bed. Florence suspected that Matthew was not going to school and was hanging out with a friend at home; she learned that he had played hooky for two weeks. Florence called a social worker at Children's Village and said she couldn't handle him. Elaborate arrangements were made for him to return to Dobbs Ferry in late

October for a month or two, but he was kept there for only a day. When Florence's children exasperate her, she threatens to send them back to their foster parents. "Mommy, you shouldn't be saying that," Crystal tells her.

Crystal did face up to the necessity of bringing her son to live with her. In the Bronx, no one walked him to school or had any time for him. Little Daquan had misbehaved in his second-grade class. He had rolled around on the floor, quacking like a duck, and hadn't done his schoolwork. When Crystal tried to discipline him, over the phone, he had said "Mommy's only blowing off hot air." When he used words like "butt," she thought of the Hargroves and of how children didn't use rude words in Mrs. Hargrove's house. Crystal went apartment hunting and, in the spring of 1992, found a one-bedroom place four blocks from Florence's apartment for five hundred and eighty dollars a month. In September, Crystal changed her work hours: instead of six-thirty to two-thirty, her schedule was nine to five. Daquan goes to school with Florence's children and is in after-school care until Crystal gets home. He had been left back in the Bronx, and after moving in with his mother he began to repeat second grade in Brooklyn. He spends a lot of time with Florence's children, frequently sleeping over at his grandmother's apartment. Crystal often finds herself telling him,

"Daquan, I ain't your friend, I is your mother," but she is glad to have him home. "I only beat him on his behind or his hands," she says. "I don't hit my baby on his face." Little Daquan (Crystal has had his birth certificate changed so that he is now Daquan Jefferson instead of Daquan Drummond) seems at ease with Crystal's beaux, who sometimes sleep over, and he visits the Bronx with her regularly. She often teases big Daquan, who is still attracted to her and keeps in his closet some of the clothes she wore when they met. "They his memories," Crystal says. A combination of her teasing and her need for money recently conspired to make her decide to go to bed with him, but at the last minute she backed out, and later told a few friends that she wouldn't "do the nasty for twenty-five dollars." Crystal warns little Daquan about taking up with women like her. She has modest expectations for him. "If he brings me a high-school diploma, I be satisfied," she says. "The one thing I know is he ain't going back to foster care."

Pamela, the social worker at the Center for Family Life, left for another job in September, 1992. She had worked with Florence and her children for a year and a half, but she had been unable to budge Florence on the issue of corporal punishment, which Pamela opposed. Florence said she was going to continue to hit her children, and she did. They all know their punishment corners. And yet Pamela, who knew Florence's faults, thought she also knew her strengths. "I think that she has potential and that the kids may do all right," she said in January, 1993. "Despite all the history of foster care, they really are a family."

AFTERWORD

Washington, D.C.
April, 1993

Of all the people I have written books about, Crystal Taylor is my favorite. It is a balmy evening and I am smiling because I have just spent an hour on the telephone with her. I even smile when I dial her number or when she calls with some news. It has been three months since the two-part article about her and her family appeared in *The New Yorker* and tonight I had to choose a title for our book. One afternoon in August, 1991, Crystal had told me about her family's eviction from the apartment on Sheridan Avenue when she was eleven. She, Florence, Carlos, and Matthew had spent a month after the eviction living in the basement apartment of a drunken friend of her mother's, where they had had to use candles because the electricity had been cut off. It was then that she quoted the two lines of a poem by Langston Hughes, which appear on page 35. A week before tonight's conversation I obtained a copy of "Mother to Son" and sent it to her. "Yeah," Crystal said, as soon as I brought up the poem. "That's nice. That man writes like I talk, using ain't. And lookit, I put an extra *s* on stair. When you was up here last month and we had dinner, you told me how much you liked my extra *s*'s."

[173]

"You're right," I said. "Whenever you talk about your lingeries or your mens, it's so much more original than the way I speak." I had the same feeling when Crystal spoke of blousing through magazines I browsed through and when she wrote, in a diary she kept for me while I was out of the country at the end of 1991, "Money is the sauce to all evil traits."

"Well, for all the hanging out we done we neither of us ain't made much progress language-wise," Crystal replied. "You's still saying 'asked' and I's still saying 'axed' but it don't matter. I'll learn you one of these years. Call me next week. Love 'ya. Bye."

Is There No Place on Earth for Me ?

"[A]n extraordinary act of journalism."
—*Washington Post Book World*

Winner of the Pulitzer Prize for nonfiction, *Is There No Place on Earth for Me?* tells the story of how "Sylvia Frumkin," a highly intelligent young girl, became a schizophrenic in her late teens and spent most of the next seventeen years in and out of mental institutions. Sheehan follows "Sylvia" for almost a year, talking with and observing her, listening to her monologues, sitting in on consultations with doctors, and even for a period sleeping in the bed next to her in a mental hospital.

"[Susan] Sheehan is tenacious, observant and unsentimental. The history of a single patient leads us into a maze of under-staffed institutions, bureaucratic fumbling, trial-and-error treatment and familial incomprehension. Though Sheehan keeps herself invisible, her sympathy is palpable."
—*Newsweek*

Psychology/0-394-71378-8